PODGE & RODGE

The

Ballydung

Bible

PODGE & RODGE

The Ballydung Bible

DEDICATED TO THE MEMORY OF PETER ALEX O'HARA.

Who helped put the 'O' in O'Leprosy.

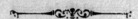

Compiled By: Ciaran Morrison, Mick O'Hara and Maia Dunphy

Published in 2007 by Solo Books
info@seminalmerchandising.com

ISBN 13: 978-0-9552968-1-9

Authors: Podge & Rodge

Photo credits: O'Hara, Wilson, Morrison, Dunphy, Rafferty family archive.
Special Photography: Ronnie Norton for Norton Associates.

Illustrations by Bruce Ryder
The Golden Arse illustrated by Pete Marry

Thanks to Ronan McCabe, David Bell.

Designed by Gary Kelly and Steve Averill at Four5one Creative, Dublin.

When I was asked to write a foreword for The Ballydung Bible, I immediately said no and changed my phone number.

But after some quiet contemplation and a small bribe received in the post, I thought - why not? We Irish carry a lot of baggage, some more than others, and I thought maybe a book is exactly what those dirty little devils need to exorcise their demons and indulge in a little self-help. Knowing them as I do, I should have known better. Exercise their demons and indulge in a little self-love more like! Because what you have in your hands is everything you always wanted - but probably never needed - to know about Podge & Rodge. There are no other two souls like these bawdy brothers on this fair isle (or any other for that matter), but by delving into this book, you might discover some interesting facts about what makes them tick, enjoy some prose worthy of Behan, and find out for yourselves how the brothers from Ballydung became the bitter, twisted and resentful little gobshites that we all hate to love today.

Go on; turn the page at your own peril!
Sinéad O'Connor

WHAT YOU HAVE IN YER FILTHY PAWS IS
'HISTORY', WELL 'HIS' STORY AND 'MY' STORY TO
BE EXACT. FOR THE FIRST TIME WE'VE DECIDED
TO OPEN UP THE DOORS TO BALLYDUNG
MANOR AND GIVE YA THE KEY TO OUR HOME
TOWN, SO YIS CAN ROAM AROUND AND STICK
YER NOSES INTO OUR BUSINESS.

Why? Cause we're sick and tired of the Irish paparazzi
and gutter press making up stories about me and the
brother; how we're supposed to be closet gaylords,
instead of twins. How I've sold me soul to Satan, and
that we are money grabbing, tax avoiding so and so's
and filthy perverts; only two of which are true!

We've also raided the kitchen drawers and the attic and
pulled out all the ould bits and bobs that middle aged
Irish bachelors do be hoarding and we spent almost an
entire evening gluing and sticking stuff into what yer
holding now.

So if yer desperate to get to know the secrets of
Ballydung, probe our back-story, and get stuck into our
cracks and crevices, then keep reading. But be wary fair
traveller; there's stuff so shocking in this book that it'll
straighten yer pubes, bring ya out in a rash and leave
ya with lockjaw!

YA HAVE BEEN WARNED!

Podge

I HAVE TO BE HONEST WITH YIS, THIS BOOK WAS A PAIN IN THE HOLE TO PUT TOGETHER, SO YIS BETTER APPRECIATE IT! I'VE JUST ABOUT GOT ALL THE STAPLES OUT OF ME FINGERS NOW, REMOVED THE SELLOTAPE DISPENSER FROM ME ARSE AND UN-SUPERGLUE'D ME EYELIDS.

All this 'cos the brother got fierce testy when he saw some of the stuff I wanted to put in the book.

But all the same it's turned out good and I have to say it's a bit of a stumble down memory lane. Yes, we've got lots of regrets, an awful lot of regrets, jaysus, a fierce amount of them altogether; but we decided that it was time to clear the boards and let yis get to know us a little bit better, especially any of you single ladies out there! Call me…

Rodge

The History of
Ballydung

Compiled By Gussie and Faluja Bollokin

BALLYDUNG - A REAL SHITHOLE

Ballydung, which translates directly as 'Town of Shite', was originally just a crossroads where the people of County Ring would bring cartloads of animal and human faeces to dump.

These piles of excrement were managed by the Dungsters, a group of hardy men whose job it was to grade and bag the waste for export, mainly to Wales. The Dungsters and their families built shacks and tents along the crossroads instead of commuting from the surrounding towns. And so the town of Ballydung was born.

Little exists of the original dwellings built circa 1600, as they were constructed from shite and hair. However the original footprint of those first homesteads are evident in the town centre today. In fact the famous 'Ballydung Jax' is built on the foundations of the home of what is believed to be the first resident of Ballydung, 'Ambrose Brown'.

With the discovery of coal, the arse fell out of the dung market, but the Dungsters stayed and adapted and many of our local residents can trace themselves back to the original settlers. The phrase "I wouldn't touch you with a shitty stick." was coined in Ballydung.

BALLYDUNG AS A PORT

Many stories have been told about the year 1901 when Ballydung's worst Mayor ever; Boozy D'Organ decided that Ballydung should avail of a grant by Westminster to help set up ports in Ireland. The residents of Ballydung got behind him, bought fishing vessels and pleasure boats and set up marine shops undaunted by the fact that Ballydung was 170 miles from the nearest coastline.

NIXON'S STOOL

Nobody can forget the proud day that the 37th President of the United States himself stopped in Ballydung and took a dump in our village on his way from Shannon to Dublin. Barney Pollop was a witness on that famous day.

"I was cutting me hedge, and up pulled an entourage of big black cars and fellas on motorbikes. It looked like something from a filum. Then out jumped yer man Nixon, I couldn't feckin' believe it! Now he looked a bit sweaty and I heard him utter to one of his CIA fellas "Cover me, I gotta drop a load!" And like a fella much younger than his years, he leapt over the wall and into Queelan's field. As he grunted, I snuck around and took a closer look. There he was - the President of America with a cigar in one hand and a bunch of dock leaves in the other. He wiped like a leader, I'd say it was spotless! Then in the blink of an eye, he hopped back over the wall and off they sped; totally unaware that there was a witness to the Presidential pile." recalled Barney.

People came in their droves to see the most famous stool in Ireland, and luckily, local historian Doctor Freenum was on hand to preserve the Commander in Chief's steamer, which is proudly displayed to this very day in the Town Hall.

To commemorate the great event, 'Nixon's stool' was built by local carpenter Donny Gussit with a grant from the Heritage Council, and was officially placed in the famous field by snooker player Ray Riordan in 1973 for all the family to sit on and enjoy.

The saying "I'm off to the oval office to take a Nixon" is still used today.

BALLYDUNG ASYLUM

Like all landlocked towns in Ireland, Ballydung was a haven for the 'madness'. So in 1778 Ballydung Asylum was built by a British Professor of the Clinically Insane, Walter Nobscaught, who whilst on tour of mad towns of Ireland was astounded at the sheer levels of insanity. Many theories were bandied around at the time as to why there was such a high level of lunacy in Ballydung; from contaminated dung water to high levels of inbreeding.

And so the most secure asylum in the British Isles was constructed and filled with crazy townfolk. At this time, it is believed that there were more people in the asylum than there were left in the town. A lot of people claimed to be mad, just to look inside the building. But despite Professor Nobscaught's intervention and attempted cures, the poor man himself fell foul of the madness and died in 1787 in a bath of milk, convinced he was Cleopatra herself!

It wasn't until the 1900's that mental experts from around the world came to the conclusion that people in the Midlands in Ireland weren't technically mad, but simply fuckin' depressed and bored off their tits.

Our most famous residents, Podge and Rodge O'Leprosy, were committed back in 1936 and remained on after the asylum was officially closed with the last of the inmates known affectionately to the boys as 'Granny'.

In 1959, the property was renamed Ballydung Manor and it and its demesne is currently owned by the O'Leprosy brothers.

THE SLAUGHTER HOUSE

After the failed attempt at becoming a port, Ballydung became famous for farming and killing things. Ballydung Bison is still famous in many Eastern European spots to this day. The slaughterhouse was built by Ballydung Co-Operative in 1974 with money from the EEC. Unlike the rest of Ireland at this time Ballydung prospered as this killing house became the pride of the Midlands. The sheer volume of animals butchered was unrivalled even by the Russians.

But once health and safety regulations were introduced in the eighties, hundreds of penalties were issued by the Department of Health after the discovery of unwanted pets, diseased livestock and the odd human ending up in the mincer.

Several scenes from the 1977 Charles Bronsan feature film Deathwish 9 - Murder in the Abattoir' were shot in the slaughterhouse.

In 1984 Colostomy Meats (A German company) took over part of the original building and to this day produces quality meats, but on a much smaller scale.

The remainder of the building was converted in 1992 and became Ballydung multiplex, which proudly boasted the minimum two screens allowed to qualify as a multiplex. However with only one projector now working, its status as a multiplex is in doubt.

Charles Bronson himself was invited to open the cinema, but said he was busy and didn't fly economy. 2FM star Electric Eddie cut the ribbon instead.

The Hanging Tree

A double bill of 'Sister Act' and 'Cannibal Holocaust' was the first presentation.

PUBICON CREAMERY

Owned by the Pubicon family, the Pubicon creamery is the Midland's premier creamery, producing milk, butter and cheese products all with that special Pubicon taste. With over two hundred years of dairy farming behind them, the Pubicon creamery (after the Slaughterhouse) is Ballydung's biggest local employer.

THE TOWN SQUARE

Ballydung is a market town and its square still holds its market every Tuesday morning where people can buy everything from pirated DVD's to pirated sportswear, fruit and vegetables to crack and cocaine.

The Town Hall dates back to 1880 and was built by Lord Fanshaw as a gift to the town for sparing his life during the Midlands Uprising of 1875. It now houses the Mayor's office, the Ballydung STD clinic and the House of Wank adult store. Back in 1989 the Town Hall housed the ill-fated Ballydung Waxworks, which opened the summer of the heat wave and resulted in a number a children being treated for shock after seeing the grotesque half melted human effigies of their favourite stars in all their skin peeling horror!

Next to the Town Hall is the Ballydung shopping arcade which is home to fashion shop 'Blue Jeans', 'Doggy Doo's' pet shop, 'Orang-u-tan' for all your tanning needs, and the tattoo parlour 'Show us yer Tats.'

On the opposite side of the square is Fidl, where everything's cheaper, Freenums Pharmacy and Fancy Goods and Sheila's. Sure we've all been in Sheila's. Then there's our famous three pubs in a row 'The Shitty Stick', 'Bollokin's' and biker bar 'The Jap' formerly 'Howard's bar'. And right in the middle of our town square is the famous Ballydung Jax, the oldest public toilet in the world, which is quite fitting when you think about the origins of our town.

LOCAL SURNAMES

Anally	Goggins	O'Pluracy
Ballsac	Goolick	Phlegm
Bollokin	Hump	Pollop
Brown	Manson	Potter-Pube
Bulbous	McArsagon	Pubicon
Coque	McCracken	Queelan
Cyst	McGee	Rash
D'Organ	McGut	Rancid
Eczema	McLusty	Roids
Fitzgiblets	Mingus	Scratcher
Fitzgoolies	Ni Gurk	Stenkirt
Fitzgoolygans	Ni Scrollock	Splatter
Fitznobs	O'Ganky	Squitters
Freenum	O'Hairy	Swillshank
Fudge	O'Hernia	Swollocks
Funt	O'Hoolican	Whank
Gakalon	O'Length	Winfrey
Gawkin	O'Leprosy	
Girth	O'Mong	

SURROUNDING TOWNLANDS
NEIGHBOURING VILLAGES

ABBEYSPHINCTER	DONG	NIPPLESTOWN
BALLYBOLLOK	FIDDLERS MINGE	RASHRING
BOGNOBBER	FLAMING HOLE	SMELME PASSAGE
BROWN LOGS PASS	FOUR SKIDS	SQUITTERS BRIDGE
BUMFORD	GOBBLERS NOB	THREE MILE HOLE
CASTLEBARETHIGH	HEEHAW	TOOLEND
CASTLE COLON	HOGGERS HILL	WANKLESBRIDGE
DEVILS HORN RIDGE	MULLINASNOT	

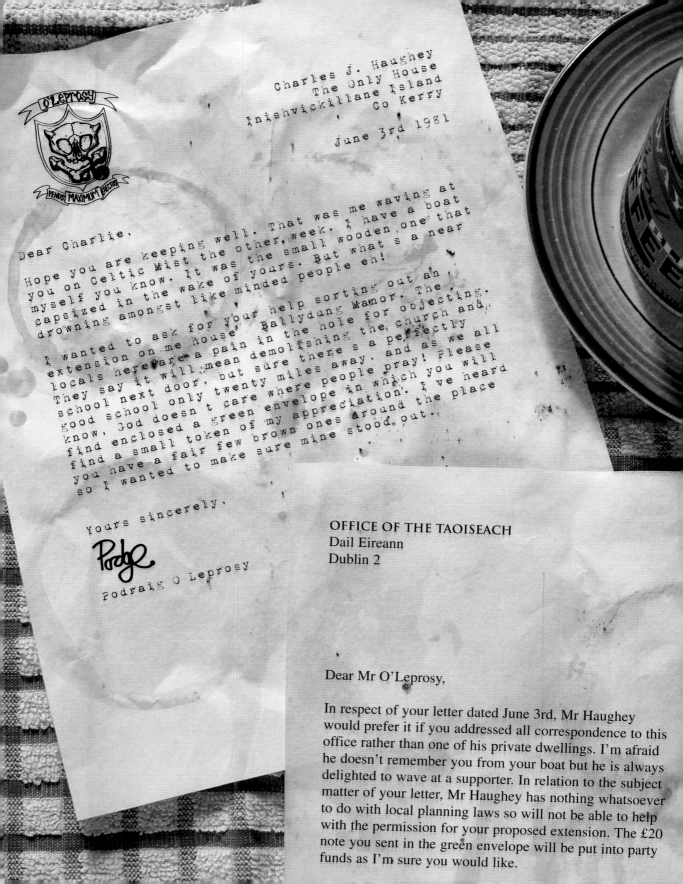

Charles J. Haughey
The Only House
Inishvickillane Island
Co Kerry

June 3rd 1981

Dear Charlie,

Hope you are keeping well. That was me waving at
you on Celtic Mist the other week. I have a boat
myself you know. It was the small wooden one that
capsized in the wake of yours. But what's a near
drowning amongst like minded people eh!

I wanted to ask for your help sorting out an
extension on me house, Ballydung Manor. The
locals here are a pain in the hole for objecting.
They say it will mean demolishing the church and
school next door, but sure there's a perfectly
good school only twenty miles away, and as we all
know, God doesn't care where people pray! Please
find enclosed a green envelope in which you will
find a small token of my appreciation. I've heard
you have a fair few brown ones around the place
so I wanted to make sure mine stood out.

Yours sincerely,

Podge

Podraig O Leprosy

O LEPROSY

PENDST MAXIMUM ERECTUS

OFFICE OF THE TAOISEACH
Dail Eireann
Dublin 2

Dear Mr O'Leprosy,

In respect of your letter dated June 3rd, Mr Haughey
would prefer it if you addressed all correspondence to this
office rather than one of his private dwellings. I'm afraid
he doesn't remember you from your boat but he is always
delighted to wave at a supporter. In relation to the subject
matter of your letter, Mr Haughey has nothing whatsoever
to do with local planning laws so will not be able to help
with the permission for your proposed extension. The £20
note you sent in the green envelope will be put into party
funds as I'm sure you would like.

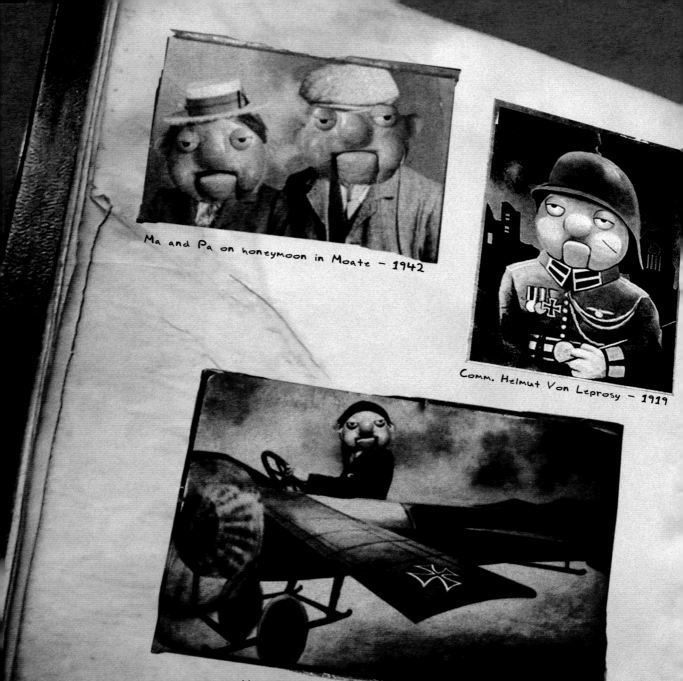

Ma and Pa on honeymoon in Moate — 1942

Comm. Helmut Von Leprosy — 1919

Young Helmut at Luftwaffe school — 1913

O'Leprosy cousins visit Australia – 1948

Podge and Rodge with Auntie Una – June 1947

Cousin Larry and his ventriloquist dog "Snaffles"

Granny Gawkin – 1943

IRISH CURSES
AND HOW TO USE THEM

EVERY IRISH PERSON WORTH THEIR SALT KNOWS HOW TO USE CERTAIN SWEAR WORDS AND CURSES. IT'S SECOND NATURE TO US. BUT FOR THOSE OF YOU WHO MAY BE NEW TO THE COUNTRY - OR JUST VISITING - HERE ARE THE MOST POPULAR IRISH PUT DOWNS AND HOW TO USE 'EM:

ARSEAGON: (arss-a-gone) (noun) someone who is a pain in the backside to have around. Arseache can also be used in the same way. Eg: "That arseagon has only gone and shat on the bonnet of me car again!"

AXE THE BACK OF ME SACK: (colloquial) (saying): please rephrase the question to the back of my scrotum. Eg: "Ya want the remote control do ya? Well, you can axe the back of me sack."

FACE LIKE A SLID IN SHITE: (colloquial) (saying): not much of a looker. Eg: "I don't fancy yours, she has a face like a slid in shite".

FECKIN' EEJIT: (fek-in-eege-it) (adj & noun): very common put down all over Ireland. Not as strong as gobshite (see below) Eg:"What kind of feckin' eejit is he? Thinking he won't get stabbed when he goes up to Dublin?"

FECKLESS ROGUE: (fek-les-rhow-ge) (adj & noun): a scurrilous individual.
Eg: "He's some feckless rogue. He's after robbing me seat while I was in the jax, and me after leaving me jacket on it!"

FISHY CACKS: (fi-shee-kaks) (adj & noun): a woman of questionable hygiene. Eg: "Howiya fishy cacks!"

FELCHMONGER: (fellch-mung-ur) (noun): a slithery sort who you don't want hanging around your neighourhood. Eg: "Did you hear they caught that felchmonger down at the abattoir with his meat in the meat?"

FLUTE: (floot) (noun): A procrastinator. Eg: "Stop acting the flute and get on with it!"

GAYLORD: (ghay-lorde) (noun): a fella who likes other fellas. Eg: "I'm telling you, that gaylord was eyeing up my mickey in the pub toilets the other night".

GEEBAG: (ghee-bagg) (noun): a woman you're better off staying away from. Eg: "Yer one's an awful geebag, she'd spit in your face as soon as look as ya."

GOBSHITE: (gobb-shy-t) (noun or adj.): a complete fool in every way. In female company, the variations 'Gobsheen' and 'Gobdaw' are often used. Eg: "Can you believe that gobshite tried to stop that moving car with his head?"

PONCE: (ponse) (noun): Not quite a full gaylord (see above), but heading that way. Eg: "Yer man is an awful ponce riding that bike with no crossbar around town".

SKANGER: (skang-ar) (noun): a little bollix from the inner city of any major town. Eg: "Give me back me phone, ya little skanger!"

SHITEHAWK: (shy-talk) (noun): a chancer, dishonest person. Eg: "That feckin' shitehawk's already been sniffing around that widow and her man still warm in the grave"

UP THE HIGHEST HOLE OF YER JACKSIE: (colloquial) (saying): you can keep your ideas to yourself. Eg: "Hold that thought and stick it up the highest hole of yer jacksie!"

WHORING BOTTLESQUATTER: (hoo-er-ring-bott-el-skwat-ur) (adj & noun) someone who's a bit pervy. There's something just not right about them. Eg: "I'm not asking that whoring bottlesquatter to my lad's first Communion."

a scare at bedtime

THE GOLDEN ARSE

WHAT THE HELL HAVE YA GOT THERE *ROBERT MUGABE?*

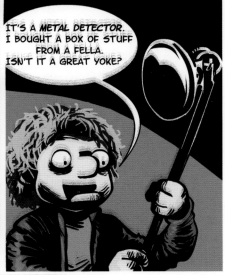

IT'S A *METAL DETECTOR.* I BOUGHT A BOX OF STUFF FROM A FELLA. ISN'T IT A GREAT YOKE?

YA SCUTTERING GOBSHEEN! THAT'S *SATAN'S TOOL* THAT IS!

I'VE GOT THE *QUARE FELLA'S* TOOL IN ME HANDS?

INDEED YOU HAVE, THAT MACHINE COULD UNEARTH DEMONIC ARTIFACTS THAT COULD POSSESS YOUR SOUL WITH A *THOUSAND CURSES.*

A *THOUSAND CURSES,* JAYSUS THAT'S A FIERCE AMOUNT!! TELL US MORE GIRLFRIEND.

LISTEN TO THIS YA MIGHT LEARN SOMETHING

'A YOUNG FELLA CALLED *PRONSIOUS NI CROTCH* HAD STUDIED ARCHAEOLOGY IN *TRINITY COLLEGE* UP IN DUBLIN.'

BAAH! WHERE ALL THE DUBLIN *PONCES* LIVE!!

SHUT UP OR I'LL CHOP THE REST OF YER TOES OFF!

HE WAS HEADING OFF TO SOUTH AMERICA ON HIS FIRST EXPEDITION IN SEARCH OF THE LOST INCA VILLAGE OF *LICKYBUMBUM.*

SOUNDS LIKE ONE OF THEM PLACES WHERE THE NATIVE TRIBESWOMEN WOULD BE WANDERING AROUND WITH NOT MUCH MORE THAN A *STRIP OF BARK* COVERING THEIR *HAIRY PARTS!*

'HE GATHERED HIS SHERPAS AND LED THEM TO THE LOCATION FROM HIS DREAM.'

DIG HERE! NOW!

'BUT THE INCAS WERE UNSETTLED.'

DAMN FOOLS!, GIVE ME THAT SPADE

CLUNK!!

'HE REMOVED THE SOIL WITH HIS HANDS. IT WAS MORE AMAZING THAN HE COULD HAVE IMAGINED. THE SOLID GOLD ALMOST BLINDED HIM.'

'AS THE TERRIFIED NATIVES FLED, PRONSIOUS WAS TRANSFIXED. IT WAS SAID TO BE FASHIONED IN THE SHAPE OF THE BUTTOCKS OF THE INCA GOD *PATA CHEEKY*.'

PATA CHEEKY WAS SO IMPORTANT IN INCA MYTHOLOGY THAT IT WAS SAID "THE SUN SHONE OUT OF HIS *ARSE!*" HENCE THE SAYING!

HAVE THOSE INCA FELLAS NOTHING BETTER TO DO THAN MAKE STATUES OUT OF FELLAS ARSES?

'AS HE LOADED UP THE TREASURE ONE OF THE NATIVES CAME OUT OF THE BUSHES TREMBLING AND WARNED HIM NOT TO REMOVE THE STATUE FROM ITS SACRED PLACE.'

BE WARNED FOR IT IS SAID HE WHO TOUCHES THE GOLDEN ARSE WILL BE CURSED OF A THOUSAND CURSES!

THAT'S A FEROCIOUS AMOUNT OF CURSES. I SUPPOSE HE TOOK THE STATUE?

INDEED HE DID!

THE SCUTTERING *GOBSHEEN!*

CURSES GET FECKED OUT THE WINDOW WHEN THERE'S *GREED* INVOLVED. NI CROTCH PICKED UP A ROCK AND *THREW* IT AT THE NATIVE STRIKING HIM DEAD!

CURSE THIS, YA NATIVE PRICK!

THE GOLDEN ARSE WAS DISPATCHED HOME BY SEA WHILST NI CROTCH FINISHED HIS BUSINESS. FOUR MONTHS LATER THE BOAT WAS FOUND DRIFTING OFF THE WEST COAST OF IRELAND NEAR *SCAB HEAD, COUNTY GALWAY.* THERE WAS NO ONE ON BOARD

HAD SOMEONE *PINCHED* THE GOLDEN ARSE?

'NO. IT WAS FOUND IN THE HOLD, OUT OF ITS CRATE COVERED IN FINGERPRINTS, THE CURSE HAD GOT THE CREW FOR CERTAIN BUT NO BODIES WERE EVER FOUND.'

JAYSUS!

THE SACRED OBJECT WAS SENT TO PRONSIOUS' HOME TOWN OF *CASTLEBARETHIGH.*

'A COUPLE OF WEEKS LATER PRONSIOUS ARRIVED HOME TO A MASS FUNERAL. ALL HIS FAMILY AND THE *ENTIRE* VILLAGE HAD BEEN WIPED OUT. THE LOCAL DOCTOR SAID "ARRRRGH" BEFORE HE TOO DIED, HIS BLOOD, LIKE ALL THE OTHERS TURNED TO *SAND!*'

OH DEAR GOD, WHAT HAVE I DONE??, THIS CURSE IS SPREADING LIKE A *PLAGUE!*

'WELL HOW COME *HE* WASN'T DEAD?'

'THAT'S WHAT PRONSIOUS NEEDED TO FIND OUT. HE WENT BACK TO HIS ALMA MATER IN SEARCH OF ANSWERS...'

ANYONE WHO TOUCHES THIS ARSE IS A *GONER!*

HOW COME *MY* BLOOD HASN'T TURNED TO SAND?

YOUR CURSE IS NOT *INSTANT DEATH.* FOR THE OBJECT NEEDS YOU TO RETURN ITS SACRED RESTING PLACE

BUT WHAT WILL HAPPEN TO ME ONCE I'VE DONE *THAT?*

'THE PROFESSOR COULDN'T ANSWER THAT ONE, BUT PRONSIOUS KNEW THAT HIS WOULDN'T BE A HAPPY ENDING. '

'SO DESPITE THE ADVICE, PRONSIOUS CAME UP WITH AN ALTERNATIVE AND LOCKED THE CURSED OBJECT INSIDE A SAFE, SO IT WOULD REMAIN UNTOUCHED FOR ALL ETERNITY.'

NOW THAT'S SMART!

OH YA THINKS SO DO YA DOCTOR BENNY BULLSHIT? YEAH A *GOOD IDEA* UNTIL IT WAS *STOLEN* BY A NOTORIOUS THIEVING GANG.

A GANG OF *ARSE BANDITS!*

PRONSIOUS WAS *DELIGHTED* TO BE FINALLY RID OF THE CURSED OBJECT. LIFE SEEMED TO RETURN TO NORMAL FOR *NI CROTCH* AND HE SWORE NEVER TO BE GREEDY *AGAIN.*

'TEN YEARS HAD PASSED AND IT WAS *NI CROTCH'S* WEDDING DAY. HIS BRIDE WAS RADIANT AND HE HAD NEVER BEEN SO HAPPY IN *ALL* HIS LIFE. THE HAPPY COUPLE SET OFF ON THE CRUISE OF A LIFETIME, PRONSIOUIS *COULDN'T* HAVE BEEN HAPPIER.'

'PRONSIOUS WAS INTRIGUED AS SHE HEAVED A PRESENT OUT FROM UNDER THE BED.'

I SAW *THIS* AND I KNEW YOU'D JUST *LOVE* IT

'THEY WERE IN THE HONEYMOON SUITE, HIS NEW WIFE WALKED OVER TO THE BED ALL SEXY LIKE.'

I'VE SOMETHING TO SHOW YA I THINK YOU'LL LIKE IT!

IF THE ROOM IS A ROCKING, DON'T BOTHER KNOCKING!

I BET HE WILL!

AS SHE LIFTED THE LID, SHE SCREAMED IN PAIN AS HER BODILY FLUIDS *TURNED TO SAND.* THE CURSE HAD CLAIMED NI CROTCH'S BRIDE.'

JAYSUS IT *WASN'T.*

IT *WAS*

THE GOLDEN ARSE!!

DID THEY NOT GET A CHANCE TO DO THE REVERSE COWGIRL? OR THE LIMBERING MONKEY?

NO

OH THAT'S A ROUGH CURSE. SO DID HE END UP BRINGING THE ARSE BACK TO INCA LAND AFTER ALL?

NO, NI CROTCH DIED OF A BROKEN HEART THAT VERY NIGHT.

THAT'S *SHOCKING!* AREN'T CURSES A *BUGGER* ON YER BACK! BUT WHAT HAPPENED THE CURSED ARSE?

'WELL, HALF WAY ACROSS THE ATLANTIC, THE CAPTAIN PASSED A CABIN FROM WHERE AN *INTENSE BRIGHT LIGHT* SEEMED TO BE EMANATING. CURIOSITY GOT THE BETTER OF HIM AND *HE TOO* BECAME ANOTHER VICTIM OF THE CURSE.'

AND DO YOU KNOW WHAT THE NAME OF THE SHIP WAS?

THE USS ENTERPRISE?

NO. *THE TITANIC!* IT'S HARD TO AVOID AN ICEBERG WHEN THE CAPTAIN'S A PILE OF SAND ON THE FLOOR!

JAYSUS!

SO WHAT *ELSE* DID YOU GET DOWN THE MARKET?

A BARGAIN. SOMETHING I'VE BEEN WANTING FOR *AGES*. A SNAZZY NEW *BIKE* STAND.

THE GOLDEN ARSE!!

Year	Artist	Description
1955	THE CLANCY BROTHERS	The only band to actually wear Aran jumpers on stage without fainting. Did us proud in the US. Their Ma's would be proud.
1962	THE DUBLINERS	Stalwarts of Irish music. Putting Ireland on the map, and making the ladies melt long before Westlife. National treasures.
1963	THE CHIEFTAINS	Paddy Moloney and the lads started a band that's still going strong today. Boys done good.
1964	JOE DOLAN	He may only have one real hip these days, but was always a national treasure .
1965	FESTER & AILIN'	Years before plagiarisers Foster & Allen hit the scene, these two brought out their single "Tropical Diseases". Way ahead of their time. The boys done good.
1968	VAN MORRISON	Believe it or not, Van the man's first album was in 1968. He's a grumpy bollix, but his ma's still proud.
1969	CHRISTY MOORE	The one man pool of sweat singer releases his first solo album. A legend. National treasure.
1970	HORSLIPS	Probably off their bins on magic mushrooms when they came up with the idea of marrying rock with trad, but the best thing about Irish music in the 70s. The boys done good.
1973	THIN LIZZY	Ireland's only black man Phillo kept music Live and Dangerous. National treasure.
1974	RORY GALLAGHER	We'd have the blues too if we came from Ballyshannon. Ah, he was a divil with the geetar. The boy did good.
1976	U2	First Bono took over the world with his unique sound, now he's trying to save it. Ireland's No.1 export. The boys done good.
1977	THE BOOMTOWN RATS	Mouthy Geldof, a fella in pyjamas and a song about Mondays. It was all great craic, til he took the Queen's shilling. But the boy done good.
1978	THE UNDERTONES	Teenage Kicks. Ah yes, we'd like to give some teenagers a good kicking too… But not bad, not bad.
1979	DON BAKER	The only man not jailed for taking his organ out in public and wrapping his lips around it. We think the boy done good.
1980	JOHNNY LOGAN	First of the Euro-wins. Can now be found flogging fast food to fat kids. But still put the country on the music map (albeit for the wrong reasons). Half way to shame·
1983	ENYA/CLANNAD	Enya leaves family band Clannad to go solo. The wily banshee is still conning the Yanks into buying her caterwauling today. For that alone, she gets points. Could be worse.
1984	THE POGUES	They broke onto the scene all those years ago and how McGowan is still alive we'll never know. But they did us proud. Boys done good.
1985	DANIEL O'DONNELL	There's something a bit odd about him, but the grannies still love Daniel. Winning the ould dear vote. Could be worse.
1986	ASLAN	The biggest band in Finglas. Their hit 'This Is', puts the boys on the map, for a bit. But you can't keep these boys down. Not bad not bad.
1987	HOTHOUSE FLOWERS	Irish hippies,there's nothing worse. The smelliest Irish band in living history. If you didn't get too close they weren't bad
1988	LUKA BLOOM	Hot on the heels of his more successful brother Christy, Kevin Moore changes his name and brings out a solo album. Like a tribute act to his infinitely better brother ·Half way to shame ·
1990	SINEAD O'CONNOR	The high priestess of Irish music had her first global hit. Mad and bald but brilliant. The permanently pre-minstrel National treasure.
1992	THE CRANBERRIES	Fronted by a whinging anorexic banshee Delores,they made it big in America, but so did George Bush. Half way to shame.
1993	BOYZONE	Stupid name, stupid band, stupid songs, stupid dancing. National shame.
1995	RICHIE KAVANAGH	A modern day poet and Seanachai. King of the single entendre. National Treasure.
1996	BRIAN KENNEDY	Although he's been around a while, his album "A Better Man" brought him solo fame. Whether or not the title referred to what he was looking for, we'd rather not know. Nothing to smile about.
1998	B-WITCHED	They were going to be the biggest girl band in the world. They weren't, C'est La Vie! Now get a life! They could have done better.
1999	WESTLIFE	How they continue to get away with it we'll never know. Cover band in suits. Nothing to smile about.
2000	BELL X1	Not much good comes out of Kildare save the horse racing. But all the young people seem to like Mr.Bell. Not bad, not bad.
2002	SIX	They had their six minutes of fame and that's all they deserved Utter shite. Nothing to smile about.
2003	DAMIEN RICE	Rice pudding!. Nothing to write home about.
2004	RONAN KEATING	After the Boyzone years, the chancer is still going strong, at least in Asia and Germany where we don't have to listen to it! Could have done better.
2006	THE BLIZZARDS	The most exciting thing to come out of Mullingar since Joe Dolan. Could be worse.
2007	DERVISH	We used to be top of our game at the Eurovision, but after this lot, we officially lost it. Who'd have thought anything could be worse than the McCauls?! National shame.
2010	THE FUTURE OF IRISH POP	With a Boyzone reunion in the air, things could go either way. The break up of Westlife could compensate. Nothing to write home about.

1 2 3 4 5 6 7 8 9 10

10: national treasure
9: boys done good
8: your ma would still be prou[d]
7: not bad, not bad
6: could be worse
5: half way to shame.
4: nothing to write home abou[t]
3: could have done better
2: nothing to smile about
1: national shame

Blazing Saddles

ARREST MADE IN LADIES' BICYCLE SADDLE SNIFFING CASE

A MAN HAS BEEN ARRESTED FOLLOWING AN INVESTIGATION INTO THE SNIFFING OF LADIES' BICYCLE SADDLES IN THE FOUR SKIDS AREA OF BALLYDUNG.

The man - named locally as Rodge O'Leprosy - was caught in the act at the newly erected holy bicycle racks outside the Church of the Dubious Miracles. A number of women had made complaints to the local authorities about damp bicycle saddles for the last number of months, despite the lack of rain, and Gardai were confused until Margo Minge of Minge Fruit & Veg saw a man at her bicycle.

"At first I thought he was trying to steal it" she said. "But as I got closer, I realised he was sniffing the saddle and licking it a bit. I shouted at him and he ran away, but to be honest I just couldn't ride that bicycle again. I felt violated. The worst part is, there have been several days over the last few weeks when I have felt a bit damp in the saddle and I just thought I'd been peddling a bit too vigorously".

Sergeant Larry Bent from the Ballydung Garda station said it was a matter they were taking very seriously.

The accused, Mr O'Leprosy

"We did apprehend a suspect, and we intend to make an example of him. The sniffing of bicycle saddles is something we do not take lightly here in Ballydung.

My own wife had her saddle sniffed only a month ago, so I'm glad we've been able to make an arrest."

The accused, Mr O'Leprosy has a string of previous convictions including driving naked from the waist down around the church car park, dipping his spoon into another man's porridge, and telling the nuns of St Phallus' convent that he had a mole in the shape of St Francis of Assisi on his backside.

He will be charged later on this week.

Central Judicial District of Ballydung

Rodge O'Leprosy v. The Women's Cycling Association of Ballydung

To: RODGE O'LEPROSY
Ballydung Manor, Ballydung, Co.Ring

You are hereby summoned and required to file with the clerk of this court and serve upon:

Plaintiff: THE WOMEN'S CYCLING ASSOCIATION OF BALLYDUNG

An answer to the complaint which is served upon you within twenty (20) days after service of this summons upon you, exclusive of the day of service. If you fail to do so, judgment by default will be taken against you for the relief demanded in the complaint.

Podge

Name: Podraig Judas O'Leprosy

Age: 65

Marital status: single

Occupation: Illegal bicycle repairs. Unqualified taxidermy. Sometime chat show host.

Height: 4 foot 6 inches

Hair: Red, all his own, well groomed with dolphin oil.

Likes: Ladies (although they don't always like him back), smart clothes (usually acquired from dead men).

Childhood:
Siblings– He was born two months before his identical twin brother Rodge. He tied Rodge to a rib with the umbilical cord on his way out (but he still managed to get out) and has therefore taken on the older sibling role.

Education – From the age of six they lived in Ballydung Asylum but were allowed out to school at St Judas National School, Ballydung. They also got some education from a psychiatric nurse whom they called Granny, who turned out to be insane herself. Podge claims to be well read and would consider himself a bit of an intellectual.

Childhood hobbies– Pick pocketing, taxidermy and thieving from dead people.

Moral beliefs: A professional pervert.

Religious beliefs: An avid member of the Church of the Dark Lord.

Hobbies? Dolphin shooting, taxidermy and collecting arthouse films.

Optimist or Pessimist: A definite pessimist. He is a miserable bollix, everything is a conspiracy and he resents other people's success, particularly when it comes to his brother Rodge.

How intelligent is Podge: Intelligent and manipulative. He uses every trick in the book to get what he wants.

Name: Rodraig Spartacus O'Leprosy

Age: 65

Marital status: Was engaged three times, but fiancees mysteriously disappeared.

Occupation: Illegal bicycle repairs and gut scraper in Colostomy Meats. Helps his brother out on a chat show. Currently long term unemployed.

Height: 4 foot 6 inches

Hair: Red, spikey, unkempt.

Likes: Ladies – of all sorts. Animal ladies, human ladies, inflatable ladies.

Childhood:
Siblings– He made it out two months after his twin Podge, and has remained under his brother's shadow ever since.

Education– Spent some time at St Judas National School, but his brother taught him all he needs to know. In fact Podge made sure that Rodge never learnt too much for fear of losing control over his sibling.

Childhood hobbies– A peeping tom, pick pocket and pyromaniac.

Moral beliefs: Rodge is a compulsive fiddler and is constantly at himself. He's not sure if he's actually ever slept with a woman or if it was just his highly sexed imagination.

Religious beliefs: Altar boy for the Church of The Dark Lord.

Hobbies: Ladies bicycle saddle collecting. Monkey collecting—he has all 160 species of primate in the attic. Other hobbies include Dolphin shooting, cat shooting, dog shooting, shooting in general.

Optimist or Pessimist: Rodge is the eternal optimist and despite the constant putting down and holding back by Podge his enthusiasm never wanes.

How intelligent is Rodge? Bordering on special needs, and is very easily led.

Rodge

Podraig O Leprosy,
Ballydung Manor
Ballydung
Co.Ring

Tel. Ballydung 666

The publisher
O Byrne Press,

Dear Sir,

Please find enclosed a copy of my latest manuscript
entitled 'The State of the Nation' for your
consideration. I am a huge fan of your company's
publications, especially last year's "From Dry Stone
Walls to Wall Street A history of the Irish
Labourer" which had me entranced.

My humble, but truly insightful tome would be a
perfect addition to your already exemplary catalogue.

My book is a factual, historical and educational
document which looks at Ireland through the ages and
today. It cuts through the shite and gets to the truth
about everything Irish, and I believe it will become a
bestseller and perhaps, one day, become part of the
National Curriculum and might learn the little
bastards something useful other than how to Bebo and
jPod!

I look forward to hearing your thoughts and when we
can start printing. I've enclosed a number of chapters,
dealing with different aspects of Irish life and our
culture.

The first chapter is A History of Ireland .

Enjoy.

Yours sincerely,

Podge

Podraig O Leprosy
MFI, OAP, VCR, hDIP

PS: Don't bother calling me between 3 and 6 next
Tuesday as we'll be out at the mart.

the state of the nation

CHAPTER 1: THE HISTORY OF IRELAND

INTRODUCTION

Why are we cursed with red hair and freckles? Why do we drink so much? Why are we such sarcastic bastards? How come we relish having a giant chip on our shoulders? What unique qualities do both Boru and Bono share? Was Queen Medbh as big a ride as Grainne Seoige? And could Cu Chulainn deliver a long puck like DJ Carey?

To discover the answers to these, and the many mysteries of our island race, we must first travel through the anals of our history.

PRE HISTORY: 0-10,000 BC.

Nothing happened during these years, as History hadn't been invented yet.

MESOLITHIC PERIOD: 10,000 BC – 2000 BC.

Back in the BC's when there was feckin' nothing but grass and sea, Homosapian na hÉireann was utterly dependant on the bounty of nature for survival. Our forefathers with their big red heads on them, soon became accomplished hunters and foragers, whilst the mná got to grips making a primitive form of tea out of bark and boiling stuff to eat whilst perfecting the art of 'giving out'. The weather was much more temperate back then and the primitive Irish walked around in the nip. This was long before gays came to our lands from Londinium*, so arses and mickeys were just run of the mill and something only the Irish Cailins were interested in.

With hands the size of shovels and mickeys the length of a curroch, the Irish male was as proud and as fearsome a warrior as you could find in any country the world over. Armed with a primitive hurley and a sliothar made out of a caramelized boar's testicle, the freckled faced, hairy arsed Irish Celt roamed the thirty-seven counties** in search of the once plentiful Gobshiteratops; a dinosaur so stupid it thought it was invisible.

Needless to say the original Irish thrived in this fertile isle of plenty; eating, shagging and drinking with not a worry in the world. It was a heathen land, but a happy land.

Archaeologists have since proven that this Mesolithic era in Ireland was one of the happiest times in our island history.

Proven in 1981 with the discovery of the smiling bog man of Navan, who had a visible grin across his petrified face and an erection that nearly cost an archaeologist his eye.'Mickey Mór' is now displayed in Morton's bar, Trim, where they've attached a bottle opener to his lad.***

But the smiles weren't to last as the Ice Age came out of nowhere and froze the holes off whoever got in its way. It was months of hardship until the ice melted during a particularly warm August in 3000 B.C.

The Irish were almost wiped out entirely and those who survived the vicious icebergs now had only snakes and Leprechauns to eat. The thick dinosaurs didn't stand a buckin' chance! It was a dark cannibalistic time that historians would rather we forget because…well, just because.

THE BRONZE AGE : 2000BC

Many years past by and the pre-historic world transformed as man discovered fire, the wheel, gambling and hooring. Battles raged all through Europinia and the Byzantines; the Egyptians and the Moors were all going mad, killing and raping and pillaging.

It wouldn't be long before our island would be a target, in particular for the Vikings who definitely had the best looking boats in Europe and the coolest horned helmets.

Around 2000 BC the Irish were slowly transforming with the discovery of bronze, which no one really knew what the fuck to do with. More years passed and eventually they started to cop on and made pots and pans and of course swords! This was the birth of the 'fighting Irish'. With a bit of booze on him the Irish male would fight over anything; women, land and the best spot on the beach.

The trademark tartan kilt and woolly mantle became a common look for the early Irish; one which they had copied off some dead Scottish fella's corpse that had washed up on a beach in Antrim. Gone was the hurley and sliothar as the weapon of choice to be replaced by big swords and round shields with "Go Home ya fuckers" written on them.****

---

* Oscar Wilde went for a long weekend in 1865 and came back loving the pork dagger!
** The counties Ring, Gee, Flaps, Masterbatoria and Genetalia were abandoned once the English language was introduced in the 1600's and we found out what they meant.
*** Admission €7. Open April to September. Under 5's free.

**** A 'Go home ya fuckers' shield was discovered on Greystones beach, Co.Wicklow in 1894.

THE RISE OF THE CELTS: 200 BC.

With no one coming to fight and contraception not even invented Ireland was growing in population and the land started to get crowded. It was only a matter of time until some cute hooer would draw a line in the sand and say, "This is mine."

And so every lad with a sword proclaimed himself King. It was chaos for a while with Kings fighting on every corner. It got so out of hand when all the land ran out that it resulted in one fella claiming he was 'King of the Crisps.' Ironically King Crisps survive to this day. At this time in history it is said that there were eighteen Kings per square mile in Éire.

Around 200 BC the 'King' craze had calmed down a bit and Ireland ended up with five provincial Kings. King MacMuck, (who was actually a pig) was recognised as the King of Meath by its people until he was eaten in a drunken riot after the Laytown races. After that the Meathians were considered to be the thickest county in Ireland, well, until comedian Frank Carson invented the Kerryman joke in 1973 and took the focus off them.

THE MINDBLOWING YEARS: 300 BC – 500 BC.

There was a lot of mystical shite going down between 300 and 500 BC with mad lads like Cu Chulainn fighting Giants, Mrs. Lir's kids being turned into swans and pots of gold found regularly at the end of rainbows. Historians believe these tales became prominent due to our climate change facilitating the growth of magic mushrooms and the arrival of hashish, brought back from a holiday in Southern Spain by Myles 'the Stoner' Toner. For two centuries of our history most of Ireland was constantly off its tits.

THE VIKINGS AND THE HIGH KINGS: 0 AD – 1100 AD.

It was during this period in our history that the most famous Irish man of all came to prominence, and he wasn't even Irish. Saint Patrick, who historians believe was probably British or French, started preaching to the heathen Celts in 432. He was a damn good storyteller and so we all became Catholic. In exchange for joining his gang, Patrick lured all the snakes off our island as they were biting cattle and being a real feckin' nuisance all over the country. Paddy died in County Down around 461 AD on March 17th and so St. Patrick's Day was invented and is still celebrated the world over by Americans and the Irish, who will believe in anything or anyone to have a day off work.

Other than the excitement of having a new religion to talk about, there was still shag all else to do and so it was almost a relief when in 795 AD the invading Vikings came for a brawl. But they had changed their name to 'The Norse' in an attempt to pull one over on us, and well, it caught us of guard for a bit and they managed to take Waterford and Limerick, which in all honesty didn't really bother anyone. But when they went for Dublin, the Irish started to get pissed off. Luckily with all the shagging during the 'boring' and 'stoner' years Irish families were huge. The population was about 52 million, so there were plenty of young willing fellas that were game for a go! Jaysus, there were battles for years, but at least it was something to get the boys off their lazy arses and out of the house for a while!

The most famous King of Ireland during these years was Brian Boru who was crowned High King in 980AD when he managed to protect Dublin and beat the Vikings back out to sea. He was a tough bollix who had four wives and everyone looked up to him. At last Ireland had a King with a name that was nice and short and everyone could pronounce. He reigned until he was assassinated in his seventies by a Viking with a grudge. But despite this, it was the end of the Vikings and their raids on Ireland. The only trace of Vikings today can be seen in Dublin with the 'Viking Splash Tour'.

For the next few thousand years feck all happened, other than petty infighting amongst the clans and provinces. Christianity continued to grow as RTE hadn't been invented, and when it was pissing outside, sure you might as well go into the church to stay dry. The stoners became monks, 'cause it was a much mellower existence and all they had to do was draw pictures in books and colour in between the lines* and occasionally build phallic shaped round towers for a laugh.

THE WISDOM OF THE NORMANS: 1100 AD. – 1200 AD.

Not much really happened until a Norman lad named Strongbow was invited over by the King. His arrival in Ireland really pissed off the English King Henry II who didn't like the Frenchies after William the Conqueror had flattened them ten years earlier at the Battle of Hastings and set up home in Wales.

Henry II sent an army over and battled with Strongbow trying to keep him in check. If the truth be known, Henry II was insanely jealous of Strongbow's cool name as people always slagged him about having a 'two' after his name. A bit like Buzz Aldrin, who will always be the second man on the moon after Louis Armstrong.

The Normans were a huge influence on Ireland, as unlike the Vikings, they were a bit more cultured. They brought with them their crafts, songs and literature that over the years became assimilated with our culture, (mind you a lot of their songs were shit and we eventually came up with our own!). They even introduced coins to the country, as before then you had to bring four cows to the pub to buy a pint.

Suffice it to say they weren't bad fellas at all, and there's probably a bit of Norman in all of us. Ah jaysus, that sounds a bit gay, but you know what I mean!

Around the 1200's the country was once again thrown into famine, coupled with a dose of the Black Death, which some English fella must have brought over. As before, cannibalism was rampant and with the snakes all gone, it was the poor Leprechauns that were hunted and boiled. The last Leprechaun in Ireland, 'Mickey McStickey'** was gutted and cooked on a spit by the Desmond family of Mallow, Co.Cork in 1195 AD. As a point of interest they used a honey and rosemary glaze.

THE PLAGUE OF THE ANGRY ENGLISH KINGS: 1200 AD – 1550 AD.

Just when we got rid of the Vikings and we were getting on great with Normans, who came in and ruined it all? The feckin' English! The last High King of Ireland; Rory O'Connor was bumped off his throne and Henry II proclaimed his ten-year-old son John as Lord of Ireland. This really pissed everybody off, as

---

* *See the Book of Kells, Trinity College, Dublin for some top notch colouring in between the lines.*

** *Mickey McStickey's tiny stockings are currently on display in The Leprechaun museum, Las Vegas, Nevada.*

nobody wanted to take any lip from a ten-year-old kid. But we were forced to put up with a number of ridiculous laws that the boy Lord decreed.

- It is herby decreed that it must not get dark before I go to bed.
- Chips must be served with every meal and greens be banished from this land.
- Dogs are cool.

Over the next while, the English brought in a load of laws and put loads of fellas in charge of loads of stuff. We now had a land full of mayors, bailiffs, lawyers and all sorts of jobs for the boys. It was truly the end of the craic!

In 1507 we had to deal with Henry the Eighth who was so enraged at being merely the eighth Henry in his family; that it made him very volatile indeed. He was such a miserable bollix that he'd cut his wives' heads off if they looked sideways at him. When he decided on a whim that he was King of Ireland, no one dared say a word against him, not even the Pope! Henry VIII will always be remembered as a notorious fat bollix, but in fairness he did invent the divorce, which we have embraced in Ireland a mere 400 years after he invented it. It's also believed that Henry coined the phrase 'giving head' but this was never confirmed.

Ironically it was during Henry's reign that he brought in the Penal Laws, which restricted Irish men having sex with their penis. It was a ludicrous law invented by Henry to try and put a halt to the now traditional large Irish family unit. But the law failed miserably as it could never be policed. 'Hedge shagging' was rife all across the country, in fact the danger element, like dogging nowadays, only helped to increase the population further.

During this time there were a few Irishman with balls enough to stand up to Henry. One lad with a very gay name; Silken Thomas started a rebellion that would inevitably end with him losing his noggin, but at least he was brave enough to give it a lash against our oppressors.

When Eighth died in 1547 even the English sighed with relief. There were a few more non-descript monarchs that lorded it over us trying to force us to be like them, but even when they brought in soccer, the subversive Irish ignored both the offside rule and handling the ball, and inadvertently invented GAA football.

ELIZABETHAN WARS: 1550 – 1603 AD.
During the reign of Elizabeth I, rebellion in Ireland was starting to kick off. Clan leaders like Shane O'Neill from Tyrone (forefather of the Sports brand) claimed he owned Ulster and brought in a bunch of Redshanks from Scotland to brawl with the English. The Earl of Desmond was kicking up a fuss down in Munster and the comically named Sir James Fitzmaurice Fitzgerald was also getting his boot in. Even the girls were weighing in, with Grace O'Malley, the only female pirate in history causing chaos from her hideout on Clare Island. This messing ended up costing Elizabeth a fortune that she could have been spending on balls, wigs, furniture and shit for her castles. Ireland was becoming a bit of thorn in her side.

THE PLANTATION YEARS (also known as the "It was a hell of a lot worse than the word 'Plantation' sounds" Years) 1600 AD – 1760 AD.

In 1603 James I became King and instead of buggering off and leaving us alone, he forced English law upon the Irish, and took Ulster for himself. A bunch of Earls decided they'd had enough and headed to Spain for holidays and never came back.

In 1641 Rory O'More decided to have a go at seizing Dublin, but someone with a few pints on him must have talked as it all went pear shaped. But it reminded the English invaders that the Irish still had a bit of fight in them. But we were soon put in our place when the notorious shitehawk Cromwell was sent over in 1649.

He killed a feck load of people and his soldiers just took land wherever they wanted. This was known as the Plantation. It was a dark time for Ireland, and anyone lucky enough to be allowed to keep a bit of land was transplanted to Connacht and Clare, yes Clare, it's a shithole now and by god, was a shithole then! Sixty thousand Irish were sent off in a boat to work on the Plantations in the West Indies. The King and Cromwell's ruling with an iron fist had well and truly crushed the Catholic Irish, and the Protestants became the bosses. By the time Cromwell had died in 1658 Ireland's population had decreased from 1,500,000 to 500,000.

For the next forty years or so, the Irish remained broken. There were more Kings with twos in their name, Charles II and James II. Catholicism was banned, then allowed back in, and then banned again. It all came to a head in 1690 when Protestant William of Orange, (who incidentally invented the fake tan), fought Catholic James II for the crown of England. The historic battle took place just outside Drogheda, very near where the Rolling Stones would play in Slane Castle a mere 300 years later. Rumours that Keith Richards actually fought at the battle have been greatly exaggerated, as he would have been way too young to actually fight. Well anyway, William won and things remained a bit dull for another while, with Catholics allowed to do feck all once again. And then to top it all; in 1740 we had another shagging famine.

THE REVOLUTIONARY YEARS: 1760 - 1900
In the year 1760, the Irish once again started getting a bit subversive. A gang known as the 'White Boys', not unlike modern day 'skangers' (but with a purpose other than robbin' cars and getting off their bins), started bullying tactics on their oppressors with the aim of getting lower rents or higher wages. At night they'd scare the shite of Landlords, Parsons and even Priests who charged high fees. But when there's one gang there are always others. And just like centuries before when everyone wanted to be a King, you were nobody unless you had a gang. There were numerous gangs throughout the land; the Bare Arsed Boys, Dexy's Midnight Runners, the Pink Ladies, the Crips, the Bloods, the Montagues and the Capulets. But infighting and ludicrous initiation ceremonies* wrecked all possibilities of a co-ordinated rebellion.

---

*   The Bare Arsed Boys initiation ceremony including kissing another fella on the lips and having yer arse shaved in front of everyone else in the gang. Homo TV fella Graham Norton's great, great, great Grandfather was rumoured to be the original gang leader.

In 1775 a fella called Henry Grattan founded the 'Patriot Party', which to the dismay of many disillusioned gang members who wanted somewhere to hang out, wasn't that kind of party. Disappointed at the lack of booze and finger food, the gang members moved on. The 'Patriot Party' attracted a more serious membership of Irish folk who wanted their civil rights back after years of oppression. Fair play to Grattan as he got rid of the Penal Laws and Catholics were once again allowed to inherit land.

In 1782 Ireland achieved status as an Independent Kingdom, still run from the House of Lords but the Catholics still hadn't a vote. A new corrupt government was set up in Dublin, with Landlords and borough owners who would sell votes for favours (a bit like nowadays). But there were still people who wanted total freedom from England. One such lad was Theodore Wolfe Tone, who despite being of Protestant ascendancy became one of Ireland's greatest patriots, and he had a feckin' cool name! If you got on well with him, he'd let ya call him 'Wolfie'. Wolfie brushed aside all religious differences and formed his revolutionary party 'The United Irishmen' to fight for a free Ireland where all classes and religions could live together in harmony. Kind of a Ché Guevara of his day.

The Brits had Tone exiled to America, but he returned to fight with French troops backing the common Irishman in a revolution for Independence.

The 1798 Uprising was a catastrophe, the French lads, like all garlic eaters were moody bastards, who wouldn't get up until after twelve, so they were sent home and it's estimated that 30,000 Irishmen and women where killed fighting that terrible summer. Wolfe Tone was caught, but topped himself so as not to give his captors the satisfaction of executing him. If only the McCauls had done us the same courtesy after their 2005 Eurovision shame!

The United Kingdom of Great Britain and Ireland came into being on the first of January 1801. Poverty in Ireland was rife, but it didn't stop us having the craic. There were festivals and fairs aplenty, there was the usual Shrove Tuesday, Mayday, The Electric Picnic and St Johns Eve celebrations and the lesser known Poke a Pig weekend and Suck a Leper day. One thing was for sure, we weren't going to let the bastards keep us down. But a new breed of patriots were gearing up for another bash at freedom, fellas like Daniel O'Connell, who was named after the bridge and Robert Emmet, an Irishman with two first names (which was a great advantage when yer spying on the Brits, "No, sorry officer, I'm Emmet Roberts, you've got the wrong fella!")

1829 was the year Catholic Emancipation was passed, which meant that Caths were at last allowed to get proper jobs; well, the rich ones anyway. O'Connell used this opportunity to get into parliament and once there, he started a real shit storm, trying to get Ireland back for the Irish.

The majority of the Irish were dependent on the land, which was a real pain in the hole when the mother of all famines struck in 1845. This was a black hole in Irish history; millions of Paddys died and the lucky ones got dysentery and plagues whilst fleeing on over-crowded coffin ships to whatever corner of the globe would have them.

Life in Ireland was at an all time low for those left behind; there wasn't a bag of chips or a plate of mash to be had and we were ruled by Queen Victoria, the ugliest queen since Queen Mong. From 1845 to 1849, there was very little craic to be had at all. Even pushing sleeping cows over could hardly elicit a giggle.

And even after the poxy famine the Landlords were still kicking tenants out of their homes for non-payment of rent. This brought about the establishment of the Tenants' League, which had a real catchy slogan called the three F's – Fair Rents, Fixity of Tenure and something else beginning with F, but I can't remember what, (not to be confused with the 'Three F's S&M club'* off Talbot Street, whose three F's we do remember – Felatio, Flagellation and Fisting).

In the 1850's the Industrial Revolution was sweeping across Europe and things improved a bit; we were shipping food over to the Brits who were off fighting with everyone else and with this little bit of prosperity, the first shops and banks opened here and of course the very first pubs, where in fact, most of the money went. Railways were built, and tea became the national drink of choice. It was also during this era that Ireland became famous for biscuits, whiskey and stout.

But even with things having some normality, thoughts of revolution were never far behind. A Kilkenny man called James Stephens, who like Robert Emmet, had two first names to his advantage, and a Mr Smith O'Brien, who had two surnames to confuse their enemies even more, started a movement to try and drum up support for a revolution. The Irish Republican Brotherhood and the Fenians were established in 1858. But dithering and dathering, false starts, no-one telling the Kerry volunteers that the dates were changed, coupled with the non-arrival of American arms shagged things right up and the Rising in March 1867 was a feckin' disaster, but as their mothers told them "Sure at least ya had a go!"

In 1869 Gladstone became Prime Minister and came up with a thing called the Land Act that helped the tenant farmers have a few more rights. Isaac Butt was an MP who came up with something called 'Home Rule' which meant that the Irish would be allowed to rule their own affairs. But Butt, a man plagued throughout his entire schooling years because of his stupid name, was a bit shy and never got anything through parliament in London. So it was up to a bunch of messers including one Charles Stewart Parnell and a fella named Joseph Biggar, to get the Irish plight noticed using the brilliantly devised 'bore the hole off the Brits' tactics. They would talk shite in Parliament all day and all night if necessary, have endless tea breaks, and 'Biggie' once famously went for an eight hour long dump, leaving everyone twiddling their thumbs. In doing so the Irish MP's annoyed the entire parliament so much that the passing of any bills almost totally ceased. It was a cute hooer of a trick that meant that the British parliament could no longer simply ignore the Irish demands. They started a movement called the Land League in 1879 to help the tenants buy their land, and since nearly everyone in Ireland was a farmer, it was a smart move towards getting support for 'Home Rule.'

---

* Admission €20, Concessions €15, OAP's €12

Parnell soon became a force to be reckoned with, and any Landlord throwing his weight around was publicly shunned; the prime example of this was one Captain Boycott, (who despite his name was a not a superhero whose powers included 'ignoring you' from over a five mile distance). He was a rogue land agent from Mayo whose workers upped and left him one day and no one would talk to him or deliver anything to his house. He ended up leaving Ireland bewildered, wondering 'what the hell just happened there?"

Gladstone was worried about Parnell's increasing popularity so he ordered that he and his pals be thrown into Kilmainham jail without trial, kind of a Guantanamo Bay of its time, but a lot colder. This was a bad move as it caused chaos throughout Ireland, kind of like when your favourite 'You're A Star' contestant is disqualified on the whim of a disgruntled judge. When Gladstone heard about the riots in Ireland he was heard to say "For fuck's sake," and he was forced to release Parnell. Finally in 1886 Parnell saw the first Home Rule bill submitted to parliament, but even though it was defeated, it was a step in the right direction.

Unfortunately Parnell's roaming mickey meant his days were numbered, and an affair with a pal's wife brought about his downfall and split the Home Rule Party in two until the 1900's. The wily British government thought that if they gave in to a few Irish demands we'd forget all about this Home Rule nonsense. They tried to 'Kill Home Rule with Kindness'* but we're Irish and we don't let things lie, and when the First World War broke out in 1914, the lads were all set to have another lash at Independence.

THE BIRTH OF A NATION 1914 - 1949
If Ireland were a baby, it was one long and difficult labour, and even at the end of it, the poor little bastard came out screaming with six of his fingers missing.

Whilst Britain was at war, which included 200,000 Irishmen joining our neighbours against the angry Kaiser, a group of volunteers back home were planning another push for Irish freedom. Brave lads and lasses including MacDonagh, MacBride, Countess Markieviez, Ceannt, Connolly and Pearse on a sunny Easter Bank Holiday Monday in 1916 took over a bunch of buildings around Dublin, including the G.P.O. And despite the dire consequences of their actions and being out numbered twenty to one, they hoisted up a tri-colour and read out the Proclamation of Independence; claiming Ireland for the Irish. These patriots had balls of steel - even the women - and despite surrendering and ultimately being executed, the Irish people rallied behind them and demanded a Free State once and for all.

After the war ended in 1918, a new, but not very excitingly named Irish assembly 'Dail Éireann' was created by a lanky yank named De Valera. Naturally this pissed the Brits right off; who the hell were these Paddys, setting up shop without permission from London?

Just like in 1916, there were plenty of Irish willing to fight and die for the cause, including Michael Collins, who later had a

Hollywood filum made about him. The Black and Tans, however, a notorious bunch of thugs whom the British sent over to quell the rebellion, merely had a tub of ice-cream named after them, by two beardy American hippies called Ben & Jerry.
A truce was eventually called and the Prime Minister of the day Lloyd George**, yet another man with two first names, but with no call to ever change them around for spying or the like, called a meeting with a bunch of Irish delegates, including Collins. An Anglo Irish Treaty was signed; it wasn't the best deal for Ireland, but it was the best on offer at the time. It meant that Ireland, despite being allowed to set up our own government, would still be a 'dominion' *** of the Commonwealth, a bit like Canada at the time, but really, who the fuck wants to be like Canada?

Unfortunately all the Treaty did was deeply divide the country. A Civil War broke out, and it was a dark and desperate time, with Irishman killing Irishman, just like in that filum 'The Wind that Shakes the Barley'. When everyone was sick and tired of the fighting, DeValera on the anti-treaty side was heard to say "Fuck this for a game of soldiers," and the fighting stopped in 1923.

The country was in awful shite altogether. But despite all the fighting and maiming, it was the small victories that the common man started to notice; tri-colours replaced Union Jacks, red post boxes were painted green, and Harry Ramsden's was replaced by Leo Burdoch's. Even 'Irish' was recognised as an official language.

Finally under Dev in 1931, London passed a statute, which meant that legally the Irish Free State could challenge the dodgy Anglo Irish Treaty.

In 1937, De Valera managed to abolish the oath to the King who quite frankly was too busy sticking it up Mrs Simpson**** to really care. So the Constitution of Ireland was drawn up, for better or for worse, encompassing the 26 counties that to this day make up the Republic of Ireland. And we had our first ever President voted in by the people; a fella called Douglas Hyde, who was the founder of the Gaelic League. A kind of modern day High King, if you like.

So there ya have it, our own colourful, if depressing history. Now ya won't learn this kinda stuff in school! Actually ya would have, in History class, but most of yis were off your tits on E or texting yer mates during the classes or have forgotten it at this stage!

---

* Not a song by The Fugees.
** His band Lloyd George and the Commotions had several minor hits in the early 80's.
*** The British were great at coming up with new words that always meant the same thing: "You're still our bitches"
****As in Edward and Mrs., not Homer and Marge.

Old Irish Medical Cures

by Dolores Gakalon
(7th daughter of a white witch)

WARTS

There are many treatments for warts. From licking toads eyeballs to concoctions of snuff and spittle. From rubbing a penny on it and putting the penny at a crossroads. But by far the most effective cure is kissing the fifth daughter of a red headed Mother of five. However if that doesn't work touch it off a dead person.

MICKEY RASH

A mickey rash is never fun and every fella will want a quick cure for an itchy lad. There are many to choose from but an old favourite is to dip it into boiling mustard and chicken fat, wrap it for a week in stickle back leaves (also known as Sticky Willy) and then expose it to the next full moon.

MELANCHOLY

To get rid of melancholy, you must steal from the butcher's shop a piece of very lean meat, which must

then be rubbed on the forehead from left to right. The meat must immediately be buried, and as it is, you must say "As you rot so depart my melancholy."

GOUT

Back in the old days the proven cure for gout was to circle your belly seven times with an ashen faggot. But in the era of sexual correctness we would recommend the following; tie a sprig of sage to both knees and swallow a dram of cod's liver followed by a shot of whiskey and coal dust. Repeat three times daily until symptoms disappear.

BLOOD POISONING

Place a badger in one's pocket and run in a circle three times on hearing the first cuckoo of the year.

IMPURE THOUGHTS (MALE)

Break an item of blessed pottery on Good Friday. It is believed that each shard will pierce the penis of Judas Iscariot.

IMPURE THOUGHTS (FEMALE):

Sit on a fresh slice of turnip whilst eating the husk of a soft cheese.

CONSTIPATION

Free your bowels with this nifty cure; pluck the feathers from a chicken's wing, place three of the feathers in a triangle, spit in the middle, then take the spit and rub it on your anus and you'll be free come the morning.

CANKER

(Mouth Ulcers): Take some gun powder, two tablespoons of baking soda, add a drop of paraffin and mix into a creamy consistency. Rub it on the soles of your first cousin's shoes.

LOCAL BOYS DONE GOOD

Interview by Phelim Quick. Photograph courtesy of Ballydung Garda Station

I WAS LUCKY TO GET TO SIT DOWN WITH BALLYDUNG'S BEST KNOWN EXPORTS SINCE THE ILL-FATED REUSABLE CONDOM - PODGE & RODGE - FOR A CHAT ABOUT LIFE, LOVE, THEIR INIMITABLE STYLE AND THEIR RISE TO FAME FROM A HUMBLE - AND POSSIBLY CRIMINAL BACKGROUND.

Your shooting-star rise to C-list celebrity status must surely come with a price. How has it affected your day-to-day lives? Privacy issues? Being mobbed outside the Ballydung Londis?

PODGE: It did. It came with a hefty price; but no one's paid it yet. We're still waiting for the million euro contracts, endorsements and the ladies that go with it!

RODGE: In fairness Podge, I was offered that deal with the intimate wipes people.

PODGE: Until they realise the wipes would dissolve on contact with your intimates ya filthy gobsheen.

RODGE: Fair point….

PODGE: Privacy has never really been an issue, as no one really knows

where Ballydung is. And even you were brought here blindfolded in the back of that horse and cart, so our location will remain safe.

RODGE: That's more to prevent the authorities and taxman from tracking us down though, rather than fans.

PODGE: And we don't have Londis down here in Ballydung. Being mobbed is not usually a problem as I

LOCAL BOYS

carry a hittin' stick everywhere I go and Rodge smells so bad, only buzzards can get within 5 foot of him.

RODGE: That's true enough.

You've brought your search for women on the road with your Desperate for Housewives stage show. These days, do you find it harder to discern whether a woman really fancies you, or whether she just wants to bask in the reflected glow of your fame and fortune?

RODGE: What fortune? Who's paying us?

PODGE: Umm….no one Rodge. Don't worry your stinking disproportionate head about it.

RODGE: Podge gives me a generous allowance of €4.50 a week -and some small change in foreign currency - so that covers me for essentials like tea, free travel brochures and a reach around from Dirty Dora once a month!

PODGE: If he was the richest man in the world, he'd still have to pay for it! Now I have a bit of class - I'm lord of the manor, and all the ladies love a lord.

RODGE: Sure just look at Mickey Flatley!

PODGE: Bad example Rodge.

RODGE: To be fair Podge, you've been single for a while yourself.

PODGE: That's because I'm choosy Rodge. I'm waiting for Ms Right. In fact, if any interested ladies are reading this, please come along to our find a wife night…I mean show in Vicar Street. I'm not as fussy as I may first appear - if you've three holes and a heartbeat you could be in with a chance!

RODGE: Doesn't sound too choosy to me…..

If and when you venture away from The Manor, do you have an entourage / security detail?

PODGE: As I said, just me hittin' stick and the smell of benjy off Rodge. That keeps trouble makers at bay.

RODGE: As for an entourage - is that French for a threesome by any chance?

Do you intend to change your 'farmer chic' style for a more modern look in a bid to find a couple of wives? Where does your style come from? Do you look after your looks?

DONE GOOD

PODGE: Well, we get all our clothes from dead men.

RODGE: We usually wait until the day after the funeral out of respect, and then go around and take their clothes.

PODGE: My style icon would be Hugh Hefner - smoking jackets and slippers - the height of sophistication!

RODGE: I guess my style icon would be…well whoever I nicked the last batch of clothes from.

PODGE: We don't really spend a huge amount on clothes. We got a bit of an allowance for our TV show, but I took that a bit personally as if they were saying our own clothes weren't good enough. So we spent the money on whiskey and a couple of sides of beef and just wore our clothes inside out for a week. They never noticed.

RODGE: We do have a couple of tuxedos we pinched off that lad Louis Copeland.

PODGE: Of course. Good auld Louis makes a nice auld tin of fruit! They're great for sneaking into funerals of folk you didn't know.

RODGE: The funeral crashers eh!

PODGE: When it comes to looks, I wouldn't be a big man for the toiletries now. They're for ponces and ladymen! I don't know what's happened to the Irish male. Gone are the days when a bath a month would do any man.

RODGE: In fact, that still does us Podge. Although, I've heard there's a new moisturiser with a hint of tan out for men I'd like to try.
(Podge glares at Rodge menacingly)

Looking sharp in front of a live audience must present its own sartorial challenges – what "look" do you favour? Partridge Sports casual / Tubridy Tweed / Kenny Blazer etc

PODGE: We'd rather not take fashion tips from any of that lot thank you. Tubridy has a corduroy combo for every day of the week! You can't take style advice from a man who wears corduroy underpants and plays jazz!

RODGE: And Kenny takes his "look" from Sadolin.

PODGE: No, our look is unique. It's Lord of the Manor and Gobsheen of the Gate Lodge.

Accessories? Do you ever feel the need to add some bling to your look? And if so, what would you tend towards?

PODGE: Again, Ireland's gone pure mad with male accessories - the man bag? The only thing a man bag should be used for is to beat its carrier around the head.

RODGE: I do have some lovely leather accessories.

PODGE: Oh why don't you tell the good people all about those Rodge?

RODGE: Well, there are some trousers, wristbands, a neck cuff and a very nice mask….

PODGE: That's a gimp outfit Rodge.

RODGE: I was wondering why there were so many openings!

Buttock-lifts? Botox? Laser-hair removal? Have either of you indulged? Or do you have strong feelings about tampering with god's canvas?

PODGE: I think I'm pretty much perfect the way I am.

RODGE: What about that enlargement you were talking about.

PODGE: Shut up Rodge…..

Hopes, dreams, ambitions, plans for the future? To become surrogate parents? To build a fabulous deck out the back-garden?

PODGE: You couldn't build anything out our back. The graves make the ground very uneven.

RODGE: We have a water feature though. Well, it's a burst pipe we never bothered to fix, but it's very nice to look at. Except the jacks won't flush now.

PODGE: We're thinking about renting out part of the manor as a B&B, so we may need to get a couple of rooms fumigated - is that an ambition?

RODGE: Ultimately I'd like to meet a nice girl, settle down, and still keep in close contact with my dear brother Podge.

PODGE: Ultimately I'd like to see Rodge dead.

O'LEPROSY

Messers Podge and Rodge O'Leprosy,
Ballydung Manor,
Ballydung, Co. Ring,
Ireland, Europe.

AIR MAIL

Kurt Mingus
Apt. 32/16
Loftus Heights
31st Street & Ninth Ave,
NYNY106314
New York

Dear Messer's Podge and Rodge,

I hope this letter finds you well. You may not recognise my surname as the Mingus clan emigrated from Ballydung in the 1850's. And even though I've never been there, I feel a strong bond with the old sod. That's why I've decided to contact you directly.

You may not be familiar with my work, but I am a best selling author here in the U.S specialising in biographies, in particular; famous Irish personalities. And since you're probably Ireland's most famous duo and from my ancestral home, I decided that you would be the subjects of my next publication, which is near completion. I was hoping for your co-operation in authorising this currently unauthorised biography entitled 'Podge and Rodge Exposed' to be published by Cox and Whine' books.

Please find a draft enclosed and feel free to make notes on any facts, dates, events you may recall differently, as accuracy is something I pride myself on. However, you should be aware that if you decide not to authorise this book, I still intend to publish with or without your consent.

Please return the draft with any amendments you may have in the S.A.E provided.

Yours sincerely

Kurt Mingus
Author

PODGE AND RODGE ~~EXPOSED~~ GAY TITLE Come up with something BETTER!

offered sex for sale, but that was never proven.
Hooreen, now pregnant with twins, did however marry
the man she believed to be the father.

Phelim Rua O Leprosy born 1896, was the thirteenth
son of a thirteenth son. The family dated back to the
original Dungers of Ballydung and owned a small
farmland on the outskirts of the town. Phelim was a
farmer/~~undertaker by profession. And it is~~
~~interesting to note that he was stand in State~~
~~Executioner when Mr Pierrepoint was unavailable.~~
~~Records show that his annual income for this position~~
~~was 1£.~~ Little else is known about Phelim who liked
to keep to himself and rarely spoke to anyone.

Phelim O Leprosy and Hooreen Gawkin were wed on
September 2nd 1942 in the Church of the Dubious
Miracles ~~after plying the priest with drink to sign~~
~~the registry~~ papers.

Six months later, on the wettest day of the year and
on the stroke of midnight Podraig Judas O Leprosy was *
born in the O Leprosy kitchen. It is rumoured, but
cannot be substantiated that Rodraig Spartacus
O Leprosy was born a full month later than his
brother Podge. Local midwife and voodoo practitioner
Urina O Hairy was unable to confirm this fact. A
submission to the Guinness Book of Records was made
by an anonymous local in 1955, requesting Hooreen be
included in the category of Longest Labour however
insufficient evidence resulted in its exclusion from
the record book.

*Add in - making him technically a bastard

Very little is known about the O Leprosy boys' early
years since most townsfolk are afraid to talk about
them, as both brothers — particularly Podge — hold a
lot of sway in the town. Podge was ~~self appointed~~ elected
Mayor for five years in the early nineties. I did

however manage to meet up with an old neighbour of the
O'Leprosy's, Mrs Ni Scrollock, who was more than
willing to talk about the infamous family. "That
mother of theirs was a dirty woman and the Father had
them hollow eyes, bulbous and heavy lidded, and had a
permanent sly look on him. No one has a good word to
say about that family around here! As for the twins,
Mrs Ni Scrollock looked visibly shaken. There was
something wrong with that pair from day one! They were
born under an eclipse of the moon, some say Rua wasn't
their father at all, that it was Satan himself that
seeded them! They burnt my house down! And did ya know
their grandfather was a Kraut? He fought for the
Kaiser! Devil Nazi little evil bastards, they are! And
they burnt me house down! And did I tell ya they burnt
me house down?"

FUCKIN' BITCH!

But it's hardly any wonder that the O'Leprosy brothers
grew up perverted and twisted. Their father, Phelim,
spent more and more time away from Ballydung, up in
Dublin on official business. When hanging became
less popular; Phelim made the fatal mistake of taking
his work home with him. When they dug up the six acre
field in Ballydung, the police found fifty two bodies
all with broken necks. The police report concluded
that O'Leprosy had been hanging random crime suspects
off his own bat. He hanged them at night up on the
hill off the old oak tree.
He was charged with multiple murders and he himself
suffered the same fate as his victims, as Phelim
O'Leprosy was the last man to be hanged in Ballydung.
My sources tell me that Hooreen fell back into her
old ways to make ends meet, leaving the young boys at
home to be looked after by their grandfather Helmut,
who had an infamous rage, a clawed hand, and a hatred
of all living things.

Brilliant and gifted

LIES LIES LIES
replace with 'father was a Postman'

You're a dead American!
You will die for calling our Mother a hooer!

GAMES WE USED TO PLAY

As vetted by Podge & Rodge

MAIM THE NEW BOY:

An old school yard favourite all throughout Ireland in the 1940's, where it was common practice to inflict serious bodily injury on an unsuspecting new pupil. A sort of painful welcome to our school. Many lost an eye, but they gained a classroom of friends. Popular maims included: Chinese mickey burns, red hot bottle cap to the face and removal of a little toe.

KICKING THE CAN

Suitable for one to as many as ya like. Not much to it, other than kicking a can really. In the days before PSP.

PISSING IN THE POST BOX:

Much more popular when the Post Boxes in Ireland were painted red and owned by the Royals, but there was nothing more fun when we were growing up than perfecting yer aim from a standing position and getting it right into the slot, then waiting behind a bush for the post man to arrive for his four-thirty pick up.

DIGGING UP A CORPSE

A game suitable for any number of players. Must be played at night. Not much point to it really, but it was better than sitting at home in the days before telly.

DING DONG SHIT BAG:

A classic. Fill a paper bag with dog shite, leave it on someone's doorstep, set fire to it, ring the bell and run away! Watch from behind a hedge whilst your neighbour tries to stamp out the doorstep inferno thus spraying hot poo all over his feet!

RIDE A COCK HORSE:

If you know what this game is, then you were in the Ballydung Scouts between 1964 and 1971 and there's no need to explain. If you weren't, there's no need for you to know.

STONE SKIMMING

Skimming stones on the water.

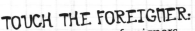

TOUCH THE FOREIGNER:

We didn't get many foreigners in Ballydung, but when one did appear, we'd have great craic altogether. You'd have to hide, and then leap out and touch the foreigner when he walked past. Extra points if you touched his face or he bit you.

BARE ARSED BARBED WIRE:

A local favourite where ya had to climb over the fence at the back of the Pubicon Creamery without shredding yer arse cheeks. It was the ultimate dare. Later replaced in the Seventies when the Creamery installed an electric fence by the even more painful 'Bare Cock Electric Shock'.

PISSY IN THE MIDDLE:

Someone's in the middle of a circle, and everyone in the ring takes a piss on them. Not so much a game as a fun way to pick on someone you didn't like.

DOG SHITE DERBY

Before the days of pooper scoopers, Ireland was littered with dog shite. In Queelan's lower field we constructed an obstacle course of dog turds. Two 'doggers' were blindfolded and had to race each other across the track on all fours and the one that was covered in the least amount of shite was the winner!

LANDMINE CHARLIES

A great game dating back to the First World War. Ya need a big field. Ya dig a bunch of holes in it, fill each hole with piss or poo, cover them over with grass so they're invisible and two teams go 'over the top' at each end of the field and see which team has the most survivors.

BOMBS AWAY

Stand on a chair with an empty biscuit tin a couple of feet in front of you on the floor, clench a stack of coins between your arse cheeks. Spread yer arms to form wings and when your ready shout 'Bombs away', jump off the chair and release the coins over the target. The player with the most coins in the tin, wins the pot.

STINK FINGER

Form a circle of players, each must stick their finger up your arse. Then in turn each player must say this tongue twister "Inger linger stinky finger, tinker ringer winker stinker" The first person to make a mistake gets stinky fingered on the face by everyone else and is out. The speed that the tongue twister is recited must increase as the rounds continue. Last man standing wins.

Farmer Sutra

The ultimate guide for the lusty farmer

THERE ARE MANY SEXUAL PLEASURES TO BE FOUND IN AND AROUND ANY FARM. FOR THE FIRST TIME EVER WE REVEAL THE SECRETS OF THE FARMER SUTRA.

CHANGING THE TRACTOR TIRE
(also known as the 'Zetor Wetter')

The use of a tractor's mechanical form can be very beneficial to any sex act. The woman wearing only a pair of wellies faces a rear tire to get a grip on the rubber treads. The male enters from under the woman's mudguards with his 'jack' and pumps until fully inflated.

THE MUCK SPREADER

Deemed to rude for even this book!

HERDING THE COWS

For the farmer who has a 'herd'. All female partners must choose a room in the farmhouse as the farmer roams the 'field' with his stick at the ready. One by one he rounds up the 'herd' and corrals them into the bedroom for cross breeding.

THE SHEEP DIP

Choose a good looking sheep and dip away.

MILKING THE COW

The farmer gets on all fours, his partner sits on a three legged stool and releases his milk. Note: A milking machine can be used by the bachelor farmer for the same effect. However extreme caution and the lowest possible speed on your Fullwood Packo is recommended.

W4 NK

GREASING THE HOE

The female should be in her open position, with extra lubrication. The farmer should be at least two hay bales high off the ground and ready for entry. He should leap with abandon onto the greased-up Hoe.

PULLING THE PLOUGH

The female partner ties bailing twine to the farmer's 'ripened stalk' and begins ploughing with vigour. Once the 'plant' is ready to seed, the 'stalk' should be immediately coupled with the female 'thresher box.'

SUCKLING THE CALF

Requires a large breasted partner. The woman lies on a table frame with 'teats' hanging downwards. The farmer or 'calf' lies underneath and suckles at will. Sting and Trudie are alleged fans of this one.

CROP ROTATION

This one's all about planting your seed in different areas. Before climax, prepare to distribute your 'seeds' over as many different parts of the woman as possible. Goggles for the lady are advisable.

THE WEATHER 'VEIN'

An outdoor treat. The woman must sit astride the farmer's weather 'vein' and spin around according to the direction of the wind. Let the elements take you to heaven!

DAYLIGHT SAVINGS

As all farmers know, maximising daylight is important. So ease yourself in where the sun don't shine. Extra lubrication required for this one.

COCK CROW

One for the early riser. At the first light of day, the farmer assumes the 'proud cock' position and enters from behind. The woman pecks at the ground and splays her feet like a chicken. Surprisingly arousing results.

THE A-Z PODGE & RODGE

A

Arsegone - one of Podge & Rodge favourite phrases.

A Scare at Bedtime – Podge and Rodge's first television show.

B

Ballydung - the lads' hometown.

BDR – Ballydung Radio 69.9 LW – Home of radio bingo and the deaths.

Bennys – Mickey lovers.

Bollokins – Ballydung's oldest pub.

C

Cocknorris (The Town of) - Ballydung towns arch rivals! Unbeaten in inter town hurling!

Colostomy Meats – Ballydung's largest employer.

D

Dunger – a native of Ballydung.

Dubious Miracles (Church of The) – Ballydung's Catholic Church.

E

Enya – No1 in the Guantanamo charts.

F

Fester n' Ailin – Ballydung's most famous musicians.

Freenum, Dr. – Podge and Rodge's doctor.

Feckless Rogues – Podge's favourite saying.

Feltcher's Holy Well (St.) - said to cure all skin ailments.

G

Granny - nickname given to the asylum nurse who raised the lads.

Gee Gees (The) – Ballydung's very own all-jockey Bee Gee tribute band.

Gawkin – Podge and Rodge's Mother's maiden name.

Gicker – Your 'swiss roll'.

H

Hardpaw - Rodge became the first human ever to catch this canine disease.

Hanging Tree – Where many met a grizzly end at the hands of hangman Phelim O'Leprosy.

Hooreen – Podge and Rodge's mother.

House of Wank – Ballydung's famous sex shop.

I

Iva Browner – Rodge's fiancee, who mysteriously disappeared.

J

Jock rash – an ailment that covers 70% of Rodges body.

Jax – Ballydung jax is the oldest public toilet in the country.

K

Kurt Mingus – deceased New York journalist and mickey lover.

L

Labia's Takeaway – Ballydung's only chipper. Home of the famous juicy Labia wedges and the Jackie Chan burger.

M

Manor - the boys' not so stately home.

Minge Fruit and Veg Shop - Does what it says on the tin.

Mickey Lovers – Bennys.

Matt Mongey – Host of 'Milk the Cows' BDR's famous Breakfast Show.

N

Nixons Stool – To mark the spot where the famous President dropped his load.

O

O'Leprosy - Podge & Rodge's proud surname .

Orang-U-Tan – Ballydung tanning salon.

P
Podraig - Podge 's real name.

Phelim – Podge and Rodge's father.

Pox the Cat – Podge and Rodge's favourite pet.

Pubicon Creamery – One of Rodge's former employers. He was fired after the incident with the mickey and the churner.

Q
Farmer Queelin - a local of Ballydung, and supplier of bacon to the Manor.

R
Rodraig - Rodge's real name.

S
Spunky the Monkey – Rodge's favourite monkey.

Sheila's – Best shop in Ballydung.

Scutterin' Gobsheen – Rodge's favourite saying.

Saddle –as in sniffing.

T
Tam Pon – Ballydung's Chinese restaurant. Chicken Balls a speciality.

Travel Vag – An essential portable device for all men.

U
Udders – Used by the Pubicon Creamery.

Under the Mattress – Where Podge and Rodge keep their money.

V
Von Leprosy – Podge and Rodge's Grandfathers original surname.

W
Weather bennys - the worst type of benny.

Whank, Andy – Host of BDR's Night Strokes.

Wardrobes of my Mind – Fester 'n' Ailin's first ever single released in 1969.

White dog shit – Seriously, where did it go?

X
Xenophobia – Podge has this...bad!

Y
You'll never be Lonesome in Prison – Fester 'n' Ailin' 1989 No. 1 hit single.

Z
Zetor – A fine tractor altogether. More pull than Rodge's mickey.

Small ads

WANTED

Massey Ferguson flange and scote coupling required. Will pay top prices. Call Bill McSlurry on Ballydung 345

Chris de Burgh look-a-likes wanted for talent show this weekend! We are looking for the best de Burgh in Ballydung! Monobrow and sheet music available at venue. First prize is a signed album and a €12 voucher for Sheila's. Ring Sheila now on 082 25 61 54

Knitting pattern for jumper like the one on the telly. Will swap for the one in the butter ad knitting pattern. Drop into Mary at the crossroads.

FOR SALE

500 Hector Books - 20cent each, €7 the lot. Call Hector on 084 2344

Lindsey Lohan Real Doll – Three openings, sarcastic smile and realistic moan sounds. Only one previous owner. Pump and repair kit supplied. Offers over €200 only. Will swap for four man tent. Call Rodge Ballydung 666.

JOB VACANCIES

Ballydung's first ever Ladies Only B&B 'Chez Lez' is now open. We are looking for a reliable illegal immigrant to work as housekeeper. Lowest rates paid. Contact Podge O'Leprosy at Ballydung Manor.

Lollipop Lady wanted for Ballydung National School. Must be fast runner as school is on dangerous bend. Non-drinker preferred, but not essential. Contact: Miriam School secretary.

Video booth cleaner needed for adult shop . Must have own shoes with non-slip soles. Ring Ken at House of Wank on 089 254 .

PERSONALS

Lovely Thai lady want meet Ballydung husband you want now! Will do every need thank you, licky licky, sucky sucky for airport ticket also and passport. Contact Tina@bangkokbrides.com

Kind hearted single male seeks lady with large feet. Must be minimum size 10. No time wasters please. I will wash your socks for free and return them cleaned and ironed. Paddy PO Box 467

Lonely lady 50-something, seeks gentle gent for long walks, dinners out, good conversations, sadomasochism and friendship. Eithne at PO Box 872

Lord of the Manor seeks lady for fun nights in and out, and in and out. Podge at PO Box 666

BIRTHS - MARRIAGES - DEATHS BIRTHS

Baby girl born to Mona and Dave Lott. Mother and baby doing well. Father awaiting DNA results.

Bouncing baby boy born to Father Flange's housekeeper Mavis. Father unknown.

MARRIAGES

The proud parents of Dympna McGee are delighted to announce their daughter's wedding to Dick Full of 15 Ballydung Crescent. No one ever thought she'd get married with that head on her so fair play to Dick!

Quick annulments and divorces available with Argew & Phibbs Solicitors. Contact 457 187

DEATHS

The body found in the canal last week has been identified as that of Phil Stuffit. Could the next of kin please take this as confirmation that the missing persons case is closed as the gardai have lost their phone numbers?

Ballydung's 4th ever serial killer was executed today in the County Gaol. The event was witnessed by some of his family and two Ballydung Local Radio Breakfast Show competition winners.

We would like to apologise to the family of Tubs O'Jockery whose death we incorrectly announced in last week's Ballydung Bugle. Mind you, it'll be in next week's if you don't pay your overdue subscription to the Ballydung Bugle.

The State of the Nation

CHAPTER 2: TRANSPORT

INTRODUCTION

Way back in our history, the only mode of transport was yer feet. Everyone walked everywhere. When ya stepped out of your cottage, sure, there'd be a fella or a Cailin walking by, "Where are ya off ta?" you'd enquire, "I'm off up the road," would come the reply and off they'd saunter about their business. Nowadays when you dare venture out you risk being ploughed down by a boy racer off his gick on E, or at the very least be subjected to his delinquent pals spotty, brown hole pressed up against the passenger window as they scream at ya "Eat me hole, ya paedo prick!"

Modern Ireland has never been more congested with our big fat EU roads crammed with gas guzzling SUV's, NCT barely made-its and bank cocks' sports cars all stuck in ten mile tailbacks, rush hour crawls or the never ending plague of road works.

Then there's the public transport system. With bus Nazis and their no change policies and their looks of glee as they plough past ya in their overfull double decker as you stand in the pissing rain at a bus stop with fifteen other unfortunate bastards trying desperately to get to a job they hate. There's nothing that gives a bus driver more of a horn than speeding past a bus stop full of eager passengers with an 'Out of Service' sign on.

Oh, and here's the answer to that age-old question? "Who the fuck would want to do such a thankless task as referee at weekend sports fixtures all over the country?" Well, look no further than off duty bus drivers! They don't give a wonky bollix how much people hate them, in fact they feckin' relish it! They feed off the power of making people's lives miserable!

Of course the trains are no better. Full to the brim with the ever-expanding waistlines of the great unwashed, crammed in like sardines shuddering towards our cities from the ever-expanding waistlines of our towns. Where once there were fields there are now millions of pre-fabricated, identical housing estates stuffed to the gills with poor bastards that can no longer afford to live any closer than fifty miles from their workplaces. Forced by circumstance to spend six hours of every day getting to work, before doing any work! And then they wonder why their kids don't know who these strange people are who appear at weekends. And if you're unlucky enough to board a train after the first two stops, get ready for a lifetime of deep vein thrombosis from standing in some cramped corner of a carriage for the entire boring journey, breathing in breakfast farts and halitosis and having to endure the 'tik, tik, tik' of the brain-dead half-deaf and their poxy j-pods set on shuffle, with every ill chosen song pushing you one step closer to going 'postal' as you fail, yet again, to complete the 'retarded' version of Suduko in your morning paper.

Then there's the Luas, ah, the Luas, let's spend all the taxpayers' money building a train-like thing for the Dubs. Just when we were putting all that 'thick Paddy' shite behind us a bunch of politicians build two train lines that never the twain shall meet. And who in their right mind would

ever go to Tallaght? As for Sandyford…what the hell is that?

And just to make up for all the overspending on road improvements, tunnels that aren't tall enough and the poxy Daniel Day,* we have a country blighted by Toll Bridges! Excuse us, but haven't we paid our car taxes, overpriced insurance and the unholy scam that is the NCT and then THEY expect us God fearing Irish citizens to pay some foreigner Toll Bridge Company to drive across OUR country? That's taking the piss directly from your bladder that is! They should be paying us two feckin' Euro to have to drive within a two mile radius of dumps like Drogheda, Ringsend and Blanchards-fuckin'-town!

---

* *Luas, ya gobshite!*

FROM A TO GEE

When we were growing up in Ballydung ya walked everywhere, there was no other option. That was the way it was all over the country. Some fellas used to ride on large dogs or fat cats, just to pretend they were getting somewhere faster, but they just looked fuckin' stupid. There was one man in Ballydung who had a horse and cart who'd bring people with money to mystical places called towns. But that would cost ya an arm and a leg and as young lads we could never afford something so extravagant. However there was a cheaper alternative in Ballydung. He was a big fella called 'Donkey' who had grown huge due to an overactive thyroid condition. He'd carry ya on the hump on his back wherever ya wanted for a shilling. But you'd have to be careful not to touch his ears as this sent him into a rage. Ironically Donkey's days were numbered when farmer Queelan bought a real donkey and hired it out for the same money. Poor ould Donkey found himself out of a job and he ended up leaving Ballydung to join a travelling freak show. His act was 'lifting things' and every showtime, he had to lift ridiculous weights. Unfortunately his back literally snapped as he hoisted a JCB above his head. Last we heard he had changed his name to Mr.Backsnap and continued to perform with the freak show until his untimely demise in 1972 after an altercation with The Mighty Lobsterman over Miss Enormarse.

Queelan's donkey 'Satan' was a miserable creature altogether but it was Ballydungs main mode of transport for a number of months. If you needed to get somewhere and bring any kind of load back with ya, Satan was yer only option. That was until one fine day when Clem D'Arcy arrived home from London with a rash and a contraption called a bicycle. People from miles came to see 'the local bike.' Initially no one, including Clem had a bog how the shagging thing worked, but once Clem got his balance, he became known as the 'Masterbiker.' A tag that stuck with him long after he'd stop riding.

Soon the whole town had bicycles, sure jaysus, you'd go everywhere on yer bike; up the road, down the road, across to there and over to yonder. It was boring as fuck, but at least ya felt you were going somewhere. But ya had to be extra careful if you went riding past Queelan's field as Satan became insanely jealous and would ruck anyone that passed by on a bike.

The first car arrived in Ballydung in the early 1950's. That changed everything. It weighed a feckin' ton, spluttered out black toxic fumes as it trundled along through main street Ballydung at three miles an hour. It was a marvel to behold and was owned by Billy Colostomy, whose Father owned Colostomy Meats. Billy was a notorious shitehawk of the highest order, and if he caught ya sniffing around his car or god forbid touching it, he'd cut your hands off and grind them into that week's mince. We soon realised that unlike bicycles, cars had the advantage of being pussy magnets, which when your hormones were raging like ours at the time, is a big plus. We noticed how all the girls wanted to get with Billy just to sit in his car! If Billy Colostomy (who not only looked like a boiled ham, but smelt like one too) could get his end away with any girl in town just 'cause he had a car, then all us ugly pricks were in with a shot. It was a revelation, and owning a car became a priority! Cars were not just about getting ya from A to B, oh no, they were for getting from A to Gee!

CONCLUSION

And so gone are the days when you'd all gather in a group and stand looking at the one car in yer town with no-one ever driving it anywhere. The glory years of driving whilst spewing black ozone murdering smoke out of the exhaust of your clapped out heap of a death trap without giving a second thought to the environment. Au revoir to the years when speed limits were more of a suggestion than a rule, and if ya got in trouble, sure a bottle of whiskey to the police station would suffice to clean yer yearly slate of offences. Gone too are the days when the greatest deterrent to boy racers were roads so shit that the potholes around every corner acted as gravelly speed bumps, ever ready to mangle their steering system and shake loose the turbo foil that they had fitted to look more like Knightrider. A time when wearing seatbelts was gay and the more kids that were hanging out the windows screaming and waving at passers by as you speeded down a back road with no markings and only enough room for half of an oncoming vehicle was considered the 'buckin' craic.'

No more can you sit on a train and have a chat with a fella out for the day from the mad house going to visit his Granny up in the 'big smoke' with no one else on the train but a stray dog that sneaked on and has been pissing up and down the aisle marking his territory. And you can forget jumping on the bus without paying and playing musical chairs, sneaking deck to deck to confuse the old conductor until it's your stop.

But despite everyone owning better cars, better roads, more public transport services there are lesbian nuns, let's be honest; ya can still get nowhere in a hurry! In truth, even with all these contraptions and timetables, we are really no better off, than we would be walking.

And did we mention the toll bridges?! Bastards!

O'LEPROSY

PENUS MAXIMUM ERECTUS

Ballydung Manor

SHIT JOKES WE FOUND FUNNY IN THE '70s

WHAT'S BROWN AND HIDES IN THE ATTIC?
THE DIARRHOEA OF ANNE FRANK.

DID YOU HEAR ABOUT THE ONE-ARMED BUTLERS?
THEY CAN TAKE IT BUT THEY CAN'T DISH IT OUT.

WHY SHOULD YOU NEVER REPLACE YOUR SANDWICH
TOASTER?
BETTER THE BREVILLE YOU KNOW...

MOTHER SUPERIOR CALLED ALL THE NUNS TOGETHER AND
SAID TO THEM I MUST TELL YOU ALL SOMETHING. WE HAVE A
CASE OF GONORRHOEA IN THE CONVENT.
THANK GOD SAID AN ELDERLY NUN AT THE BACK.
I'M SO TIRED OF CHARDONNAY.

WHEN WAS BUDDY HOLLY'S FIRST SMASH HIT?
3RD FEBRUARY 1959.

HOW DO YOU KNOW IF YOU'RE AT A GAY PICNIC?
THE SAUSAGES TASTE LIKE SHIT!

THIS MORNING ON THE WAY TO WORK I REAR ENDED A CAR
WHILST NOT REALLY PAYING ATTENTION.
THE DRIVER GOT OUT.. HE WAS A DWARF.
HE SAID I'M NOT HAPPY ...
I REPLIED WELL WHICH ONE ARE YOU THEN?

WHAT'S A JEW'S BIGGEST DILEMMA?
FREE PORK.

WHERE'S THE BEST PLACE TO HIDE MONEY FROM
A TRAVELLER?
UNDER THE SOAP.

IF JESUS HAD BEEN DROWNED INSTEAD OF CRUCIFIED
WOULD EVERY CHURCH HAVE A POOL IN FRONT OF IT?

Visit beautiful Ballydung
in the heart of the Midlands!

VISIT Pubicon Creamery
Tours and tastings available Monday - Thursday!

⭐ ATTRACTIONS
Squat on Nixon's stool, See Saint Feltcher's Holy Well,

LEARN
About our History in the Town Hall!

10 % reduction on a session in Orang-u-Tan with this ad.

Head of Operations
NASA
John F Kennedy Space Centre
Kennedy Space Centre
Florida
U.S.A

Podge O'Leprosy
Ballydung Manor
Ballydung
Co.Ring
Eire

June 8th 1975

Dear Sir,

Please find enclosed my CV for consideration as a spaceman or spaceship driver. I think it would really suit me down to the ground, or should that be 'it would suit be right down to the terra firma!' (A bit of space humour there for ya!)

But seriously, I'd really be interested in flying up into space and doing experiments and shite that ya do be doing as I need to get away from this shithole of a town and in particular my brother, who's become a real pain in the hole as of late. In fact the more time I spend cooped up with him in our home, the more I want to kill him! Seriously I will end up slicing him up with a carpet knife and burying him in the back yard or feeding him to Queelan's pigs.

Not that that should affect your selection of me as a potential spaceman, I'm sure I wouldn't have any violent episodes with my new astronaut friends, particularly with the high dose of psychotic medication I'm now on.

It would be super if you could get me on whatever course you do be doing, training fellas up and all, and may I suggest that perhaps you could include a spacewoman on my trip. Not as a driver or anything important, that'd be dangerous, but for a bit of company for the lads on those lonely nights on Mars.

Yours sincerely,

Podge

Podge O'Leprosy

PS: Do your spaceships have a telly on board, as I'm missing The Sweeney for nobody!

PODGE O'LEPROSY C.V.

SKILLS: I love meeting new people, but I am wary of foreigners.
I'm a great talker and I'm always right.
I like reading books, particularly biographies of the great Dictators.
I own a bike (front and back carriers)

ACHIEVEMENTS: Have all me own teeth
Captain of The Ballydung debating society 1963
Winner of Ballyfree Farm's 'Name the Chicken' competition 1971

EMPLOYMENT: Self employed.
Male model – July 1960
Co-owner of Ballydung 'Just Sleeping' – human taxidermy company 1972-1974

QUALIFICATIONS: Certificate of Competence, Ballydung Business School 1956

REFERENCES: President Idi Amin, The Palace, Uganda.

John F Kennedy Space Centre
Kennedy Space Centre
Florida
U.S.A

Auto Reply from NASA

Dear Mr.O'Leprosy,

Many thanks for your interest in the NASA space programme. However we are not recruiting at the moment. Please try again at another time.

Jake Davis
Cupid's Palace
Berwick Street
Soho
London

July 15th 1975

Dear Jake,
 On a trip to London about three months ago I had
the pleasure of visiting your fine establishment. For a
fella from Ireland it was a dream come true, I had
never seen such a wonderful array of filth in all me
life.

The closest I ever got seeing a naked woman in
Ireland is those ten seconds of a boob in The
Sweeney and films about African tribes on the BBC.

But your shop was a revelation to me, an orgy for
the eye and a party for the pants if you will, and I
was wondering if I could come and work for yis as I
have a real interest in the field of filth and porn.

Yours sincerely,

Rodge O'Leprosy

PS:
Do you give staff discounts?

Cupid's Palace
Berwick Street
Soho
London

Mr. O'Leprosy,
Once again please let us state that we are not
interested in hiring you as a staff member of Cupid's
Palace. The fact that you have spent over a thousand
pounds over the last year does not mean that you will
automatically be considered for employment in our
shop.

The fact that you have written to us every week for
the last three months is a sign of someone who is in
need of some help. As we have suggested previously
there are a number of sex addiction groups in the U.K
that we would strongly recommend you contact
instead of pestering us with your requests for
employment.

Please do not send any more letters as the police
have already been notified.

Yours,

Jake Davis,
Proprietor

BALLYDUNG ASYLUM PATIENT LIST - 1957

Name	Date Admitted	Condition	Status
Philip Browner	September 1954	Compulsive licker	Broke own ribs so he could lick own arse. Do not release.
Bernard Behan	June 1951	Thinks he's Brendan Behan	Suggested release by Christmas
Dick Bent	April 1957	Kleptomaniac	Almost cured. Check pockets regularly.
Jenny Swabb	August 1955	Pregnant out of wedlock	Up medication, then release.
Giorgio Labia	December 1956	Food addict	Let the fatso out. He costs too much in food bills
Rita "Roly Poly" Felch	November 1956	Sex addict	Will end up selling sex regardless. Release.
Podge O'Leprosy	May 1948	Gooburger Syndrome & mild psychosis	Not yet fit for full release
Rodge O'Leprosy	May 1948	Gooburger Syndrome & constant arousal	Still a risk to society
Phelim Quick	February 1953	Dirty, dirty pervert	Not yet ready for release
Rusty Coque	October 1951	Thinks he's a French burlesque dancer	Nothing but a benny. Release.
Elizabeth Swollocks	January 1925	Horse fancier	Release, but to be kept away from farmland.
Andy Trout	September 1949	Compulsive wanker	Still no change. Order extra tissues.

CALLING ALL FANS OF IRISH COUNTRY MUSIC AND CRAIC!
THE BOYOS ARE BACK IN TOWN!

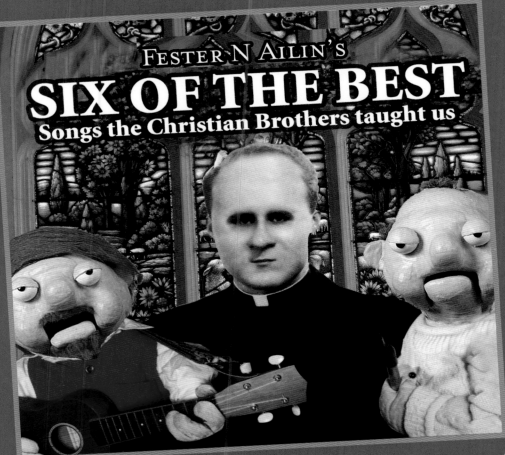

FESTER N AILIN'S NEW RELEASE IS GREAT ALTOGETHER!

That's right, they wow'd ya with their Rock 'n' Roll album, they stunned ya with their Gregorian Chants and got ya going with their Hippidy Hop album. But it's back to their roots with their latest release *(and yis will all know the words!)* it's their brand new EP of songs the Christian Brothers taught us.

Available from 'Blood on the Tracks' Ballydung Main Street' and good musical outlets everywhere.

Hear the exclusive first play on Afternoon Delight with Vince Fahey, next month on BDR!

THIS INCLUDES THE SONGS

- *DON'T TELL YER MAMMY OR YER DADDY*
- *BRING ME YOUR EAR*
- *LEATHER'D TO THE BONE*
- *STAND UP YA LITTLE BASTARD AND FETCH MY LEATHER FROM THE DRAWER, YOU'LL BE SEEING JESUS, BY THE TIME I'M DONE WITH YA*
- *CHALK DUSTER IN THE EYE*
  and the first single SPECIAL BOY (Sit on my Knee!)

BONUS TRACK
KNEEL DOWN AND PRAY TO THIS!

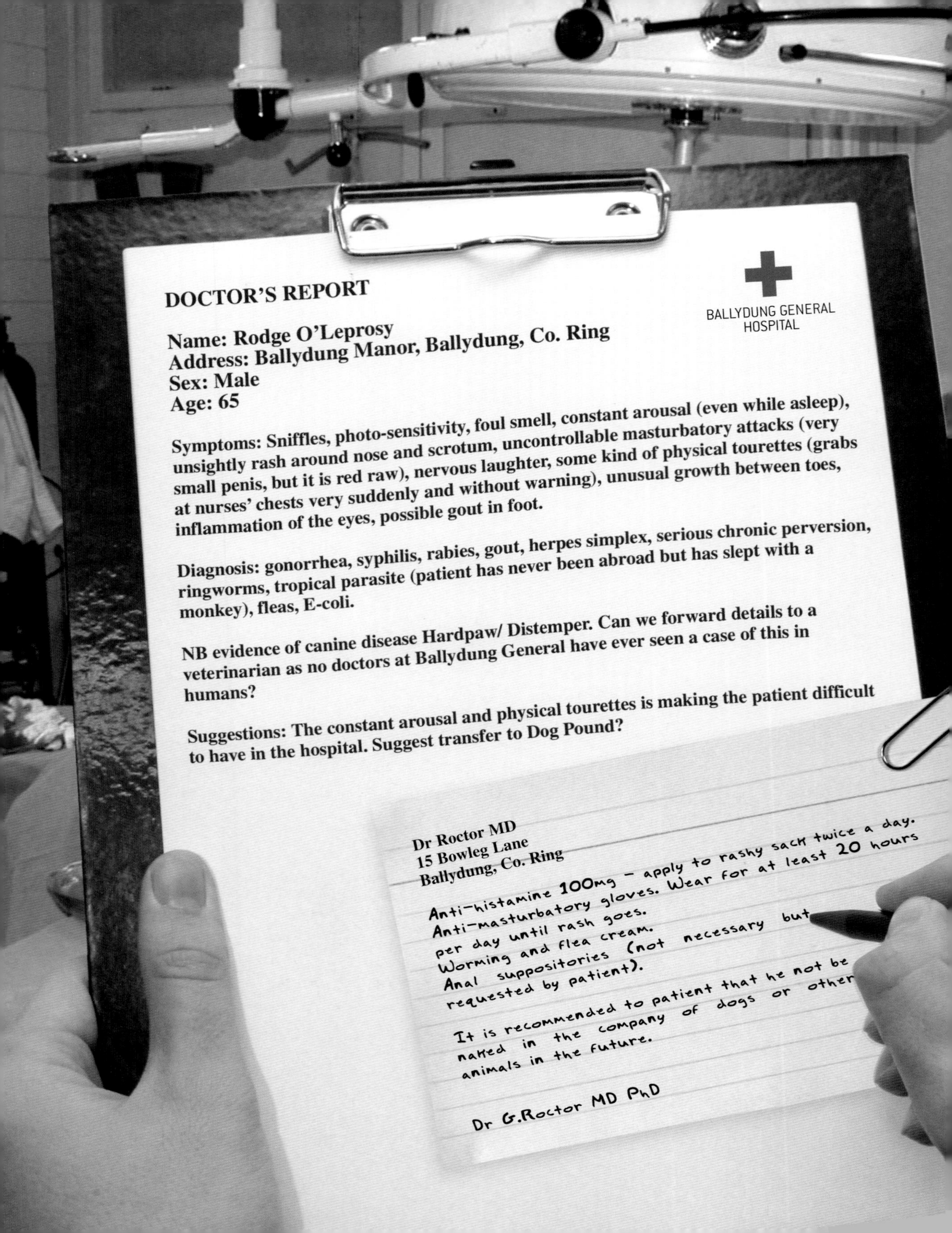

DOCTOR'S REPORT

Name: Rodge O'Leprosy
Address: Ballydung Manor, Ballydung, Co. Ring
Sex: Male
Age: 65

BALLYDUNG GENERAL
HOSPITAL

Symptoms: Sniffles, photo-sensitivity, foul smell, constant arousal (even while asleep), unsightly rash around nose and scrotum, uncontrollable masturbatory attacks (very small penis, but it is red raw), nervous laughter, some kind of physical tourettes (grabs at nurses' chests very suddenly and without warning), unusual growth between toes, inflammation of the eyes, possible gout in foot.

Diagnosis: gonorrhea, syphilis, rabies, gout, herpes simplex, serious chronic perversion, ringworms, tropical parasite (patient has never been abroad but has slept with a monkey), fleas, E-coli.

NB evidence of canine disease Hardpaw/ Distemper. Can we forward details to a veterinarian as no doctors at Ballydung General have ever seen a case of this in humans?

Suggestions: The constant arousal and physical tourettes is making the patient difficult to have in the hospital. Suggest transfer to Dog Pound?

Dr Roctor MD
15 Bowleg Lane
Ballydung, Co. Ring

Anti-histamine 100mg — apply to rashy sack twice a day.
Anti-masturbatory gloves. Wear for at least 20 hours per day until rash goes.
Worming and flea cream.
Anal suppositories (not necessary but requested by patient).

It is recommended to patient that he not be naked in the company of dogs or other animals in the future.

Dr G.Roctor MD PhD

CARDINAL **RASHERS O'LEPROSY**

Just back from the missions

PODGE ST. BOND

MODEL: Podge St. Bond
HAIR: Black
EYES: Black
HEIGHT: 6,2
BUILD: Sporty

Mooney's Models
Tullamore

EXCLUSIVE TO BALLYDUNG RADIO
- Every Bank Holiday Monday –
Podge & Rodge LIVE 6 to 9pm!

Death notices, on-air tarot readings and live exorcisms!

RESTWELL B&B
GARDENER STREET, DUBLIN 1

12th May 2007

Dear Sirs,

I'm writing to let you know that we are yet to receive the €882.16 payment from your sixteen night stay with us in April. You may not be aware but we have a policy of full payment on check out. We would like to bring to your attention a number of items missing from the room, including a mattress, all the allocated towels, the showerhead, two door handles and a trouser press.

There are also a number of items that you failed to remove from the room upon departure. These items will be disposed of if they remain unclaimed within seven days.

The items are as follows:
A greyhound, a 'Travel Vag', a collection of 'magazines', a portable DVD player with a selection of adult DVD's, a bin liner of soiled underwear, a car door from an Austin Allegro, a wooden leg and a shotgun.

Please note that we will be forced to take legal proceedings to recoup our costs. However if you have already forwarded us the cheque, please ignore this letter.

Yours,

Mrs. Nora Scuttle
Proprietor

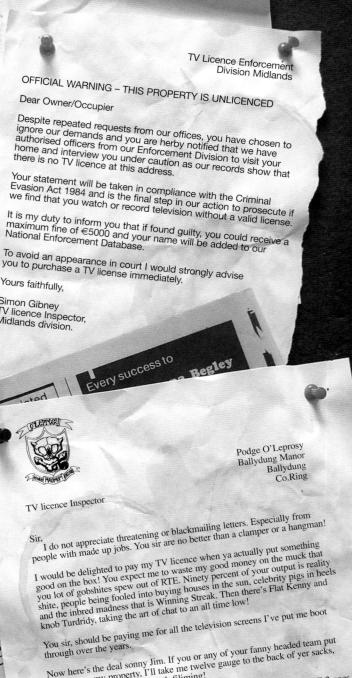

TV Licence Enforcement Division Midlands

OFFICIAL WARNING – THIS PROPERTY IS UNLICENCED

Dear Owner/Occupier

Despite repeated requests from our offices, you have chosen to ignore our demands and you are herby notified that we have authorised officers from our Enforcement Division to visit your home and interview you under caution as our records show that there is no TV licence at this address.

Your statement will be taken in compliance with the Criminal Evasion Act 1984 and is the final step in our action to prosecute if we find that you watch or record television without a valid license.

It is my duty to inform you that if found guilty, you could receive a maximum fine of €5000 and your name will be added to our National Enforcement Database.

To avoid an appearance in court I would strongly advise you to purchase a TV license immediately.

Yours faithfully,

Simon Gibney
TV licence Inspector,
Midlands division.

Podge O'Leprosy
Ballydung Manor
Ballydung
Co.Ring

TV licence Inspector

Sir,

I do not appreciate threatening or blackmailing letters. Especially from people with made up jobs. You sir are no better than a clamper or a hangman!

I would be delighted to pay my TV licence when ya actually put something good on the box! You expect me to waste my good money on the muck that you lot of gobshites spew out of RTE. Ninety percent of your output is reality shite, people being fooled into buying houses in the sun, celebrity pigs in heels and the inbred madness that is Winning Streak. Then there's Flat Kenny and knob Turdridy, taking the art of chat to an all time low!

You sir, should be paying me for all the television screens I've put me boot through over the years.

Now here's the deal sonny Jim. If you or any of your fanny headed team put one foot on my property, I'll take me twelve gauge to the back of yer sacks, now there's a programme worth filiming!

I will under no circumstances be paying a TV licence until the day RTE 2 goes porno at the weekends, Off the Rails goes nude, Kenny and Tubridy have to fight tigers in a live Gladiator style death match, yis put good Westerns on and RTE buys Marty Whelan a decent wig.

So until that day, you can stick yer licence fee right up your hole!

Have a nice day!

Podge O'Leprosy

Rodge

mammy and daddy in hell!

BY Rodge

FOURTH

PODGE AND RODGE ARE IN BED, RODGE IS BORED.

RODGE: Can I turn on the telly?

PODGE IS STARING AT A CRACK IN THE CEILING.

PODGE: No, I'm reading.

HE CLEARLY ISN'T SO RODGE TURNS THE TV ON ANYWAY. A HORRIBLE SINGING FILLS THE BEDROOM

PODGE: Jaysus what is that caterwauling?

RODGE: Oh great, it's 'I want to be famous!' D'ya know the winner gets to release their own record!

PODGE: (Sarcastic) Oh wow! What a great idea. As if the music world wasn't shite enough already. Letting desperate talentless wannabees who should be sitting behind a checkout desk or mopping the floors of porno cinema's release cover versions of songs that we despised first time around. WASTING MY FECKIN' EAR SPACE!

RODGE: I'll turn it over so.

HE CHANGES THE CHANNEL.

RODGE: (CONT'D) Oh, it's 'I'm a Hermaphrodite, get me out of here... and here!'

PODGE: OVER, NOW!

HE CHANGES TO ANOTHER CHANNEL.

RODGE: Oh great 'Erection Island' First to lose the horn, kicked off!

CONTACT

PODGE: TURN THAT SHITE OFF!

RODGE UNHAPPILY TURNS OFF THE TV.

RODGE: I don't care what you think, I'm still gonna send my tape in to 'BIG BUGGER' and become a porno housemate, and then I'll get some action for sure!

PODGE: Take that thought and divide it by nothing! If I know something, it's that you get nothing for free. Take astronaut Neil Buttstrong, he was on a one-man mission to Venus. It was all going well until he got into a spot of trouble when he hit a meteor shower and crash-landed on the surface of Venus. When Neil came to, he was amazed that he was still in one piece, but unfortunately the ship was in bad shape. From that moment he knew he was never going to get home.

RODGE: Is this going anywhere as I've got to scrape the bath out?

PODGE: Shut it you with yer disproportionate head! Neil sat in the crammed ship wondering how long he had left. Then he heard a knock on the cockpit door and nearly shat himself!

RODGE: (Interrupts) Let me guess, it was Linda Martin!

PODGE: NO. It was a hideous alien creature.

RODGE: I was right so.

PODGE: Neil had made First Contact with extraterrestrial life.

RODGE: What they had three balls?

PODGE: What are you scuttering on about?

RODGE: You said they had extra tra-tessticals! D'ya get it? Ha, ha, ha!

PODGE: I swear to you now, another one of those and I'll carve your eyes out with the leg of a stool and feed them to the cat!

Anyway it wasn't long until Neil had made Second Contact and began communicating with the Venetians they were very hospitable and despite the language barrier they seemed to understand each other. One of the Venetians clearly stood out as their leader, but because of their unearthly physique Neil didn't know whether it was a King or a Queen. Over the next few days Neil showed his new friends photographs of home. The Venetians were fascinated by life on Earth. Neil was delighted that they got on so well, he could only imagine what it would have been like to have landed on a hostile planet.

RODGE: Or Limerick!

PODGE: The next day Neil was stunned as there in front of him was a house, exactly like the one he had left behind him back on Earth. With this emotional connection, Neil realised he had made Third Contact; these remarkable Venetians, were trying to make him feel at home. It almost brought a tear to his eye!

RODGE: Benny!

PODGE: However Neil was a little confused once he set foot inside the front door. There was only one room; a bedroom. He sat down on the bed but as he did a large group of Venetians entered through the door and gathered around him. They seemed quite excited.

RODGE: What the feck is going on?

RODGE: Suddenly they all grabbed him and held him down on the bed. And as they did the Leader burst in waving a familiar magazine. It was at that moment that Neil realised two things; perhaps it wasn't such a good idea to sneak that porno magazine on board after all, and that the alien Leader was indeed a King, in more ways than one.

RODGE: Oh Jaysus.

PODGE: Yes, Neil Buttstrong was the first human to make Fourth Contact with an alien life form and was destined to live out his life as the Venetian King's sex gimp!

RODGE: Ohhh, that's gotta hurt! C'mere, what time is it?

PODGE: Arsed if I know.

RODGE: It's time for 'Midget Island'

PODGE: What?

RODGE: It's Temptation Island, only smaller.

RODGE TURNS THE TV BACK ON.

PODGE: Turn that shite off, we're watching a video.

RODGE: Oh, did ya get any new ones in?

PODGE: I did, how about Tom Crude in Position Impossible?

RODGE: Nah, don't like Crude!

PODGE: How about Gosford Pork or The Porn Identity.

RODGE: Seen them!

PODGE: Well then, how about 'My Big Fat Lesbian Greek Wedding'

RODGE: That'll do, I fancy a bit of Vagitarian!

PODGE: Sold to the man on the damp side of the bed!

THE VIDEO PLAYS. THE END

PERVI PARTY
Podge's Elected Rural Values Initiative
NO.1
PUTTING ERECTION
IN ELECTION!
VOTE PODGE

THE TRAVELLING NUN

SISTER LUGUBRIOUS

From Boston to Ballydung

This week I travelled to a small town in the Emerald Isle called Ballydung, and I had the pleasure of visiting St Feltchers Holy Well. Legend has it that back in the second century, Saint Feltcher, - the Leper Priest - whilst preaching the Good Word was attacked by a crow that tore off his weakened leper hand with his sacred rosary beads still in its grasp. But as the crow flew off the beads fell from the hand and hit the ground. And where they landed it is said a well suddenly sprung forth.

Many of the faithful have come to visit the Holy Well for many years and the water itself, despite its murky appearance has healing qualities, especially for those with severe skin conditions.

Bathing in well water has been said to cure all ailments from leprosy to scabies, from psoriasis to ring worm. Occasionally when the well gets busy, it takes on an oatmeal-like consistency and smells of dead skin.

Bottles of Holy Well water are available to buy locally or by mail for ten punts from Mr Podg O'Leprosy PO Box 666, Ballydung Ireland.

B&B's in the area cater for ski sufferers, with plastic sheeting ar moisturised toilet paper at supplemental cost, paid locally.

Next week I'm off to Scotland search of the relic of Saint Ignati and his pious scrotum.

BALLYDUNG **BUGLE**

A BALLYDUNG BUGLE SUPPLEMENT
BY PIERCE MCCRACKEN

NUMBER 631 ● NOVEMBER14, 2007 ● €1.00

IRELAND'S TROUBADOURS IN THE SPOTLIGHT SPECIAL
'FESTER 'N' AILIN'

AS THEY RETURN TO THEIR HOME TOWN, AFTER THE HUGELY SUCCESSFUL 'WHITE SUPREMACY' SOLD OUT TOUR OF SOUTH AFRICA I GOT THE RARE OPPORTUNITY TO SPEND SOME TIME WITH IRELAND'S MOST POPULAR COUNTRY MUSIC EXPORTS. BUT FIRST LET'S STEP BACK IN TIME AND SEE HOW A FARMER'S SON AND PRIEST'S HOUSEKEEPER'S 'NEPHEW' JOINED FORCES TO PLAY THE MUSIC THEY LOVE ALL OVER THE WORLD FOR THE PAST 40 YEARS.

INSIDE STORY

HOW DID YIS FIRST MEET?

Fester: We would have known one another in Ballydung National school, but wouldn't have had much to say to each other in fairness and I lived on the far side of town, and he was living in the back of the priest's house.

Ailin: Jaysus, I thought he was an awful hooer altogether, he was one of the first fellas I saw in them platform boots and the long hair.

F: Jaysus, there's not much of that left now!

A: Sure enough. But it wasn't until buckin' 1964 was it ?

F: It was summer 65. I was playing fiddle with 'Teresa and the Dandelions'

A: Oh jaysus, whatever happened to "loose legs" Teresa?

F: She's dead.

A: Right.

F: And you were playing in The Chevrolets.

A: That's right, we're on the same buckin' bill. That's the first time I knew he played an instrument, other than his flute! Ha! Ha!

F: Jaysus, we were pretty shite, mind you but we had them up sweating in fairness!

A: It was a week after that we were playing in Clonmel, but we were short a guitarist; 'cos he announced he was gay so we had to fire him, so I suggested himself.

F: That's right!

A: We played for four hours, took the buckin' roof off the buckin' place!

F: Ah, but the arse fell out of the showbands, when the roller disco came along.

A: So we decided the pair of us would have a crack at the growing Irish country market.

F: And the rest is history as they say.

'TROPICAL DISEASES' WAS YOUR FIRST BIG HIT. DO YOU EVER GET TIRED OF PLAYING THAT SONG?

A: Not a buckin' bit of it. I love it.

F: People always think that one jumped out of the box, but we had a few tunes before that one broke big.

A: 'Spread Eagled on the Hill of Clanoo'

F: Oh yeah, 'The Wardrobes of my Mind' and 'Deep in the Crevice of Love'. But I suppose 'Tropical Diseases' had the catchy chorus and the healthy message to boot.

A: I suppose it corresponded with Irish people travelling abroad for the first time.

YOU WERE THE FIRST PEOPLE FROM BALLYDUNG TO TRAVEL ON A PLANE, NEVER MIND TO LAS VEGAS. WHAT WAS THAT LIKE?

A: Twas buckin' mad altogether!

F: Good times, good times. We were hanging out with Elvis himself, Englebert Humperdink and Dean Martin.

A: Brendan Boyer was there at the time and of course the Flap Sisters, whose erotic magic act caused a sensation in Vegas at the time.

F: They were originally from Boyle.

A: Didn't you shag all of them one night?

F: I did.

WHEN DID YA HEAR ABOUT YOUR RIVALS FOSTER AND ALLEN?

A: We got word out in Vegas that there was, what I suppose you'd call a tribute act nowadays, hooring around Ireland whilst we were trying to make a name for ourselves in the U.S.

F: Bastards altogether. They stole our act!

A: Before we knew it, they had a No.1 back home with 'A Bunch of Thyme', which was a direct rip off of our song 'A bunch of Lesbians'

A: But since all country songs only have four variations anyway, we got nowhere with the courts.

F: We tried to sue the arse off them, but ended up costing us! Bastards!

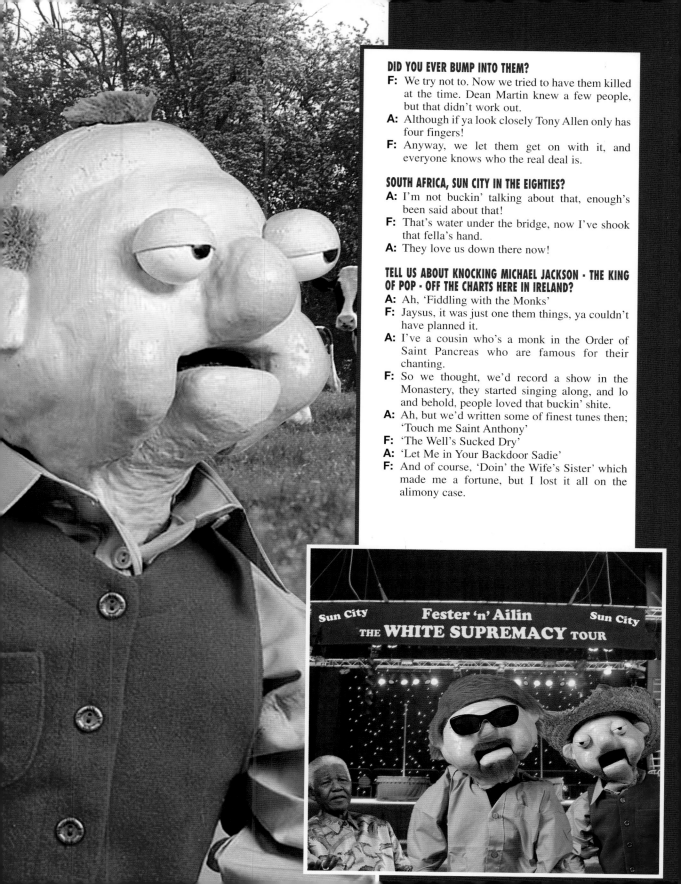

DID YOU EVER BUMP INTO THEM?

F: We try not to. Now we tried to have them killed at the time. Dean Martin knew a few people, but that didn't work out.

A: Although if ya look closely Tony Allen only has four fingers!

F: Anyway, we let them get on with it, and everyone knows who the real deal is.

SOUTH AFRICA, SUN CITY IN THE EIGHTIES?

A: I'm not buckin' talking about that, enough's been said about that!

F: That's water under the bridge, now I've shook that fella's hand.

A: They love us down there now!

TELL US ABOUT KNOCKING MICHAEL JACKSON - THE KING OF POP - OFF THE CHARTS HERE IN IRELAND?

A: Ah, 'Fiddling with the Monks'

F: Jaysus, it was just one them things, ya couldn't have planned it.

A: I've a cousin who's a monk in the Order of Saint Pancreas who are famous for their chanting.

F: So we thought, we'd record a show in the Monastery, they started singing along, and lo and behold, people loved that buckin' shite.

A: Ah, but we'd written some of finest tunes then; 'Touch me Saint Anthony'

F: 'The Well's Sucked Dry'

A: 'Let Me in Your Backdoor Sadie'

F: And of course, 'Doin' the Wife's Sister' which made me a fortune, but I lost it all on the alimony case.

HOW IS HOME LIFE NOW. AND HOW COME YOU AREN'T LIVING SOMEWHERE FOREIGN?

A: Look, we've seen the world, I've been in some of the most amazing places and women of every race and creed, but me heart's in Ballydung.

F: There's nowhere like it.

A: And there's nowhere in the world with such lax planning permission laws on this planet.

THAT BRINGS ME ON TO THE FESTER 'N' AILIN HOTEL AND CASINO COMPLEX THAT YOU ARE BUILDING AT THE MOMENT? THERE'S BEEN A LOT OF CONTROVERSY ABOUT IT.

A: Ah the begrudgers, there's always buckin' begrudgers!

F: Sure it'll be great for Ballydung; it'll bring jobs to the locals.

WHAT ABOUT THE ENVIRONMENTAL IMPACT OF A TEN-STOREY HOTEL ON THE AREA?

F: Look, with all the misery and depression in the Midlands all we're trying to do is bring a little bit of Las Vegas to spice things up.

A: That's right, and there's free drink while you're gambling; now that's a buckin' bargain if ever I heard one.

BACK TO THE EARLY NINETIES. YOU CHANGED TACK AND HAD A GO AT A NEW STYLE.

F: We're not the only ones who made the mistake of going with the trends of the day, sure look at Bono and the fellas when they went into the disco music. That was muck.

A: Look, we had been on a tour of the Irish bars in Manchester and we caught the buzz of what was going on and we thought it'd be a good idea.

F: We're not too proud to admit it, but for three of those years Ailin' used to smuggle out an accordion full of all manner of contraband.

F: I was off me tits for the whole of 1991!

A: Mind you, if you look up the internet 'Get On Your Knees and Give Me Your E's' is a cult-hit album.

F: It's going for a fortune on the eBay!

WHAT ABOUT YOUR VENTURE INTO HIP HOP?

A: Oh jaysus, you're bringing it all up, can we not move on?

F: One thing I've learnt is that the accordion does not and never will adhere to a 'beat' – it's always at least half a beat off! Which doesn't make for a good hip-hop song.

A: Mind you, you wrote some fine lyrics at the time.

F: "The bitch is a liar, the ho is a skank, she stole all my money fool, she's done robbing my bank."

THEN IT WAS BACK TO YOUR ROOTS WITH 'DOWN THE FURRY GLEN' AND THE FOLLOW UP 'WE'VE ALL BEEN IN THE ALTAR BOYS'

A: That's right, we were at an all time low, we'd lost our deal with Def Jam, and Fester had an ongoing feud with Jizzy D and his West Coast posse who apparently had a hit out on us.

F: Sure, I had a shotgun fitted to the neck of me guitar. It had gone mad.

A: We both went into rehab then back for a break to Ballydung.

F: I built a home studio and put a pole in for me new wife Clorina.

A: We got back to doing what we were good at, songs that Irish people can relate to.

F: Simple melodies and simple lyrics with a country flavour.

A: And a lesson learnt. We've never left the charts since.

With platinum discs from all over the globe and no less than four albums in the Irish Country charts at any given time. Fester 'n' Ailin will remain Ireland's troubadours for many a year to come!

FESTER 'N' AILIN

DISCOGRAPHY

ALBUMS

Fierce Faraway Places	(1971)
I've a Craving For Ya Mary McGee	(1972)
A Sack Full of Fester 'n' Ailin	(1979)
Charlton Heston Was Right	(1981)
Takin' it Up the Sax	(1982)
Live From Sun City	(1982)
Double O Fester 'n' Ailin	(1986)
Get on Your Knees and Give Me Your E's	(1991)
Ballydung Bitches and Brooklyn Ho's	(1993)
Blood on the Jax	(1994)
Fiddling with the Monks	(1996)
Another Sack Full of Fester 'n' Ailin	(1997)
Down the Furry Glen	(1997)
Live From Dunfartin	(1999)
The Green Fields of Ballydung	(2001)
My Lovely Ballydung	(2002)
Ballydung, How are Ya?	(2003)
I'm Lonely for Ballydung	(2004)
Me Auld Ballydung	(2005)
Forty Hits of Fester 'n' Ailin	(2006)
Fester 'n' Ailin – The Sun Studio Recordings	(2006)
Six of the Best EP	(2007)

SINGLES

The Wardrobes of my Mind	(1969)
Tropical Diseases	(1971)
Never Shove a Banger up Yer Arse	(1977)
There's a Dead Man up the Chimney	(1979)
Monkey Do	(1981)
My Cock Wakes Her Up Every Morning	(1982)
Doin' the Wife's Sister aka. On The Sly (U.S.)	(1987)
You'll Never be Lonesome in Prison	(1989)
Colosto You, Colosto Me	(1993)
Touch Me Saint Anthony	(1995)
Triple X Christmas	(1997)
Porno Shop Song	(2000)
A Man up the Aras	(2005)
Special Boy (Sit on my Knee)	(2007)

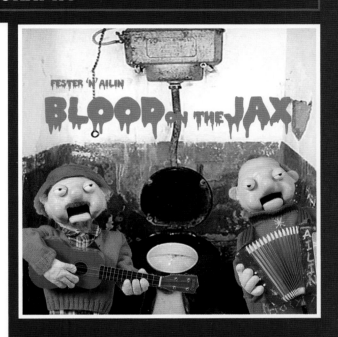

Fester 'n' Ailin

You'll Never be Lonesome in Prison

Fester 'n' Ailin
Merchandise

MUGS €12

Special Boy
(sit on my knee)

BUCKET €12

WITH DEEPEST SYMPATHY FROM FESTER 'N' AILIN

WREATH €85

FIRELIGHTERS €10

Special Wreath for a dead relative or friend

As if it came from Fester 'n' Ailin themselves

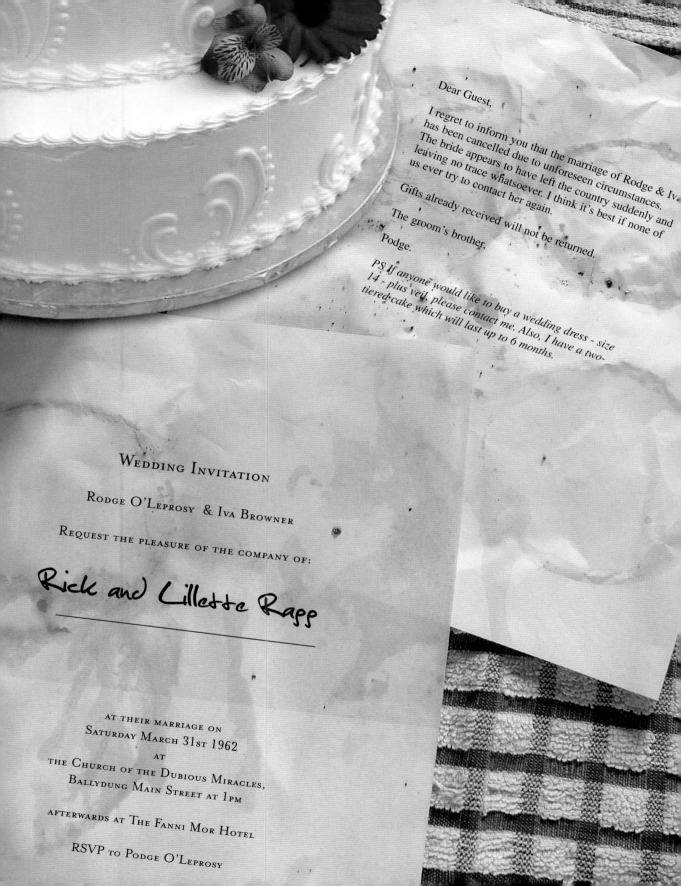

Dear Guest,

I regret to inform you that the marriage of Rodge & Iva
has been cancelled due to unforeseen circumstances.
The bride appears to have left the country suddenly and
leaving no trace whatsoever. I think it's best if none of
us ever try to contact her again.

Gifts already received will not be returned.

The groom's brother,

Podge.

PS If anyone would like to buy a wedding dress - size
14 - plus veil, please contact me. Also, I have a two-
tiered cake which will last up to 6 months.

WEDDING INVITATION

RODGE O'LEPROSY & IVA BROWNER

REQUEST THE PLEASURE OF THE COMPANY OF:

Rick and Lillette Rags

AT THEIR MARRIAGE ON
SATURDAY MARCH 31st 1962
AT
THE CHURCH OF THE DUBIOUS MIRACLES,
BALLYDUNG MAIN STREET AT 1PM

AFTERWARDS AT THE FANNI MOR HOTEL

RSVP TO PODGE O'LEPROSY

When in Ballydung Visit

GUSSIE BOLLOKIN'S PUB

Bollokin's Pub - Ballydung Town Square - Ballydung - Co.Ring
Proprietors: Gussie and Faluja Bollokin. Tel. BALLYDUNG 665

CARPET   MUSIC

SOUP

THE DAMPEST PUB IN IRELAND

TOASTIES

- AVAILABLE FOR FUNCTIONS AND OTHERS.
- CAPACITY FROM 15 TO 50
- AMPLE PARKING
- NO FOREIGNERS

BOOK YOUR CHRISTMA PARTY

TWO COURSE DINNER AND ENTERTAINMENT
FEATURING **THE GEE -GEES** (Ireland's only all
jockey tribute to the Bee Gees)

€39.99

HOLIDAY SNAPS

Ma, Pa and cousin Chuck in Moate 1947

Sitting in the famous stuffed horse of Wankilestown. The trap works, the horse doesn't

Rodge gets his first ride on the beach, Bundoran.

The boat we just missed to the Isle og Man. 1952.

Biddy Mongey's B+B famous for her ample portions.

Flasher

No1

HE RAN LIKE A BASTARD, HE RUNS NO MORE!

The world of dog racing is in mourning after the death of The Ballydung Flasher, who died in yesterdays 3.30 at Cheltenham Park. The owner Podge O'Leprosy was distraught "I had put a fifty quid on the bastard and he keels over and dies." Three times winner of the Golden Paw Award, the mutt will be missed by many. May he howl in peace as he finally catches up with the hare in the great stadium in the sky.

FARMERS' FRIEND
DIRECT FROM AMSTERDAM

DON'T DIP YOUR MICKEY INTO ANYTHING LESS

THE MISTRESS IN A JAR
PLEASE READ INSTRUCTIONS CAREFULLY

SCHOOL REPORT

St Judas National School Ballydung - Annual Report

Date of report: June 25th 1953
Pupil's name: Rodraig O'Leprosy
Class: 6th class (Miss O'Flanger)

Subjects and teacher comments:

Mathematics:	**Fail:** Rodraig has no mathematical abilities whatsoever. Even the remedial class is too advanced.
Reading:	**C-:** We had thought Rodraig might have dyslexia as his Christmas essay was about writing a letter to Satan. But he told us that was what he meant. Worrying.
Gaeilge:	**C:** Rodraig seems only to have an interest in learning curse words in Irish. But he does have a good ear for them.
Art:	**B:** Rodraig has shown a great interest in painting, and was the first to sign up for the trip to the National Gallery to see the "Renaissance Nudes" exhibition. Enthusiastic.
Sports:	**D:** Rodraig is not at all sporty and is always fiddling with himself during sports practise. He is too easily led by his brother. He can often be found holding other boys down in the changing rooms while Podraig kicks them, or steals their lunch money.
Religion:	**D:** Giving other children gambling tips on how to make the most out of their Communion money is not the kind of thing we want to promote here at St Judas'.

Head teacher general comments:
Rodraig is quite a slow child, but all the teachers feel he would do much better away from his bullying brother. Having said that, he cannot continue to bring images of naked ladies to school with him. We don't know where he is getting them, but it will have to stop.

SCHOOL REPORT

St Judas National School Ballydung - Annual Report

Date of report: June 25th 1953
Pupil's name: Podraig O'Leprosy
Class: 6th class (Miss O'Flanger)

Subjects and teacher comments:

Mathematics: **B+:** Podraig is quite good at mental arithmetic. Mainly because he operates an illegal pawn and tuc shop at break times.

Reading: **D-:** We were very disappointed that when asked to choose a novel to read this year, Podraig chose a translated version of "Mein Kampf". This is not appropriate material for an 11 year old. Can I suggest Huckleberry Finn for next year?

Gaeilge: **C-:** Podraig's insistence that Irish is a dying language is very upsetting for the whole class. Peig Sayers is an inspiration, not a 'miserable geebag' as Podraig said in his last exam.

Art: **C-:** The art teacher has said that although Podraig's artwork is quite advanced for his years, his choice of subject matter is not suitable for 6th class art. Neither is painting with faeces.

Sports: **D:** Podraig is not a team player, and cheats at practically everything. This year, 4 boys on his hurling team ended up with broken jaws.

Religion: **Fail:** Father Flange was too upset to comment on Podraig's behaviour in religion classes. He will not be allowed make his Confirmation if he continues to request the "Quare Fella" as his sponsor.

Head teacher general comments:

Three of Podraig's teachers have either left, or had serious and unexplainable accidents this year. He is quite an unpleasant child and I feel Podraig may fare better in a different school - I can refer him to Ballydung Borstal for next year.

"Ya feckless rogue!"
"Are you a benny tied to a tree?"
"Does the attic match the games room?"
"Smell my finger!"
"Cheekier than a wagon load of monkeys!"
"Don't mind if I do bartender'
'Please to meet ya, meat to please ya!"
"While you're down there!"
" Talk to the ears, cause the hand ain't listening!"
"Another day, another dump"
"Axe the back of me sack!"
"Ooh, that really stirs my broth!"
"Benny on the loose!"
"Everybody needs a bosom for a pillow!"
"Any chance of a tug?"
'That's a double flusher!"
'That really batters my sausage!
'Baths are for ponces and ladymen!
'Talk to the back of me sack!
'Ya four foot fanny head!'
'I'm as excited as Brian Kennedy in a mickey factory'

The State of the Nation

CHAPTER 3: SEX

It can't be helped; it must be done.
So down with your breeches
And out with your bum.

James Joyce

INTRODUCTION

Sex and being Irish have always been difficult bedfellows. Except for one period of our history when 'doing it' was as natural as taking a dump. However 'doing it' whilst taking a dump didn't become popular until the mid 1990's.*

Back in the time when dinosaurs and snakes covered our green isle, our ancestors wandered around naked or merely with a bit of bark covering their privates and when ya got the horn, ya had it off with whoever was standing next to ya. A bit like Tamangos in Dublin, Dazzlers in Mullingar or Rockin' Robins in Leitrim nowadays. But it all went to shite when the Catholics invaded and brought with them religion and in particular a thing they invented called 'guilt.' This was the end of free love for at least a thousand years.

Not only did St Patrick, the leader of the Caths banish all the snakes from Ireland, but along with them; the trouser snakes. The Church had such a grip on Irish sexuality that the Irish male resorted to gripping himself. With 'having a poke' banned, Ireland soon ended up with a country full of wankers, literally. Particularly in the midlands and especially Athlone.** Wexford only in the last hundred years changed its name from its original 'Wanksford.'

And since we're Irish and we take everything to the extreme; wanking soon became a huge problem. Fellas would be too exhausted to work; potatoes weren't picked because of repetitive strain injury and even the women couldn't knit after continually flicking themselves off. There was such a wanking epidemic in ancient Ireland that the river Shannon was reported by many a traveller to have flowed white with relieved Celtic man-porridge.

---

*   *Eurobrown 5' available on VHS and DVD at* **www.celtic.eros.ie**

**   *Quite a few wankers still remain in this town.*

As these 'white tides' became more and more commonplace, the Church, as usual, was there to spoil the fun! Commandment 10a. was sanctioned by Rome in 1503.

'Thou shalt not pull one's self off'

And so the Catholic Church and sex continued to be intrinsically linked for many centuries to follow, in more ways than one, but let's not get into that!

CHURCH AND MATE

By the 1950's there was no such thing as sex in Ireland. It simply did not exist. Procreation was the only reason for a man to stick it into a woman, and the quicker it was done, the better.

As a child, when you noticed a bump on your mother's tummy, it was shrugged off as indigestion. After the nine months, parents would often stage a giant fart* to explain away the disappearance of the bump. This would be followed shortly by the discovery of a baby in the cabbage patch. No wonder we were so fucked up!

The worst years were when you hit puberty; your body was transforming into adulthood, your voice dropping, hair sprouting up left right and centre and you had a sudden interest in girls. There were many questions that needed answers but no parent in the whole of Ireland was willing to give ya any. Your father would simply hit you with a stick, just in case you were thinking about sex.

For the next ten years the sexual frustration built up, fellas had to get wheelbarrows to carry around their overfull testicles. Uncontrollable erections were beaten with the back of a wooden spoon until they ebbed away. And if a girl wanted to sit on your knee at a dance she had to sit with a bag of turf between yis in case she might catch a child off ya.

And even after you were engaged to a woman, ya still weren't qualified for a touch, let alone a little 'go'. In fact, not until your wedding night was an Irish man or woman allowed to see what the other one was packing, and then it was too feckin' late to return the goods. Not that anyone ever did, because you were so excited that you were, at long last, going to actually see some flesh. After all those years of frustration and imagination you were finally going to get your end away, and it was over in thirty seconds; before you even got your trousers off!**

This kind of repressed sexuality that Ireland was forced to live under became a breeding ground for sexual deviants and filthy thrill seekers who got a kick out of breaking the rules. And there were none more deviant than ourselves.

PODGE AND RODGE GO WILD!

Growing up in Ballydung in the fifties and sixties was like anywhere else in the country; boring as shite! Except for the weekends when the ballrooms would come alive with dancing. No one really gave a shite about the music or dancing for that matter, but the primal beats, the sweaty heat and the possibility of rubbing off a girl were too much of a temptation for any red-blooded male. We couldn't even begin to count the amount of women we 'Hucklebucked' off during those days. We had special open-ended pockets in our trousers where you'd slip yer mickey out into the open and rub against any flesh that came your

---

*   Whoopee cushions were imported by the boatload at this time.
**   Wedding suit rental companies up and down the country spent thousands on cleaning trousers riddled with premature man juice for many years to follow.

way. Even another fella's* hand brushing by your lad, would give ya a little thrill.

When there was a break for tea and buns you could go out the back of the hall and meet up with Agnes Fudge, who in exchange for one tea cake would touch your mickey with a stick, and for two she would let you lick behind her knees.

THE TOP TEN SNEAKY RUB SONGS OF THE SIXTIES

1. The Hucklebuck
   Brendan Boyer

2. Brownfinger
   Billy Muff & The Jazz Hands

3. Are You Teasin' Me
   Eileen Reid & The Cadets

4. Ireland Swings
   Brian Coll & The Buckeroos

5. You Remind Me of Me Mother
   Larry Lang

6. I'm Gonna Be A Country Boy Again
   Sean Dunphy & The Hoedowns

7. Lovely Leitrim
   Larry Cunningham & The Mighty Avons

8. She Wears My Ring
   Sean Fagan

9. A Poor Man's Roses
   Red Hurley & The Colours

10. Good Lookin' Woman
    Joe Dolan

In 1969 the Captain brought back a 'Playboy' magazine that he had stolen from a GI he'd killed whilst on a fighting holiday to Vietnam. He could have gotten six years in jail for bringing something so racy into Ireland and it's understandable why.

It was the greatest thing we had ever seen; luscious nudey ladies with hairy bits printed on glossy page after glossy page! Young men travelled hundreds of miles to see the magazine for themselves, some fainting at the sheer thrill of its contents. The Captain did so well out of this one venture that he managed to purchase a car with the proceeds. It was a Ford Anglia that he called Hef, after the genius who came up with the magazine.

Since no one in Ireland would tell you anything about sex whatsoever, it was down to gossip and rumour and ultimately money that all young Irish men would find out what sex was all about. Mrs O'Flynn was a big bust of a woman from the town of Fiddlers Minge. She'd meet ya at the crossroads at 7pm and for various price points would do all kinds of deviant performances that would blow** any young man's mind.

From slapping the arse off ya with a hot water bottle to tying off your testicles with bailing twine, from sniffing her pantihose right up to sitting on yer face, she would do it all. This lusty teacher and many filthy crossroad minxes like her up and down the country provided an invaluable education to the sex starved adolescents of Ireland.

*   *This was before gays were invented, so this practice was not gay! O.K!*
**   *No.14 on Mrs O'Flynn's menu 'a blow' would cost ya six bob. And don't get too excited all she did was actually blow on it!*

Everyone remembers their first time. We set off to Dublin for our first ride on the hooers of Monto on a clear Spring morning in 1959. We were up for a GAA match, but we stayed well clear of Croker and instead waited patiently until it got dark and headed to the bottom of Mackle Street in search of a legendary woman of the night. She was an exotic woman called Fedelma and you could tell from the stretch marks around her mouth that she knew what she was doing. "Are ya looking for business lads?" she asked in a voice somewhere between Twink and Ronnie Drew. And when the street lamps caught her, she looked uncannily like a cross between the two as well. She brought us back to her lodgings, told us to strip off and slapped some bleach on our mickeys with an ould paintbrush and asked to see our money. Unfortunately we had foolishly purchased an overpriced egg sandwich that we had shared on the train journey up and we were a bit short. But in fairness she was a shrewd businesswoman and we struck a deal. Despite both of us having to have a go on her at the same time* whilst her husband peddled away at himself in the corner, it was both dirty and exciting, and we'll always fondly remember our threesome (or foursome, if you count her husband pulling off in the corner!) with the Monto Princess.

---

*   *Just for the record Rodge took the tradesman's entrance. Again, not gay!*

**   *NOW THAT IS GAY!*

THE NAUGHTIES

It wasn't until the rise in popularity of the soap opera in the 1980's that the Church finally began to lose its grip on mickeys and fannies. As Pamela Ewing sashayed across our television screens, the Irish lad's lad reawakened and the Irish Cailin saw the power that a sexy woman with big hair and even bigger shoulder pads could have over men.

And from the big haired, (in every department), Eighties came the Naughties, when we discovered that after all the years of sexual repression; many priests themselves had been 'at it' all along. At long last 'sex' in Ireland was no longer a taboo subject. Sexy Irish people came out of the woodwork and even some out of the closet.**

Today we live in a country that has a hundred satellite channels of porn from Eurosluts to Red, Hot & Dutch. The Internet is chock full of filth and fetishes you couldn't even dream up yerself. We've porn shops in every town and even your local corner shop stocks dirty rags of the highest order. Modern Ireland is a pervert's paradise. Breasts and legs are all over the place, tongue studs and butt plugs are commonplace. Modesty and good old-fashioned Irish guilt went out with the Punt.

Of course with that, the thrill of getting caught is gone. No longer do ya sneak out at night to the shed where ya had hidden a copy of 'Big Bouncing Mommas' that a fella had brought back from abroad for a sneaky midnight shuffle, no more would get a semi looking at a girl's ankle on the bus, and gone are the days of the dancehall rub. We're more open about our sexuality, more European in our views, but are we better because of it?

Nowadays the possibility of getting the horn or if you're a lady, a swampy gusset is far too easy. Sure ya can lift up the phone and call 'genuine horny Irish girls' with foreign accents and the stuff that comes out of their mouths would make Gerry Ryan blush. It was far more craic in the old days when you'd ring directory enquiries and tell the ould dear that you were 'hot for her sexy voice' and she'd scold ya down the line for being a dirty little pervert and if she found out who ya were she'd call the Gards. Now that's sexy!

The magazines nowadays have girls of all shapes, sizes, races and creeds doing stuff to themselves, to each other, to fellas, to five fellas, to their pets and to household implements. With cameras up every crack and crevice in full colour and vivid detail. It was much more of a thrill in the Seventies when the Damart catalogue came through the letterbox featuring lovely ladies in their tight cotton undies; where if ya squinted hard enough ya could definitely see bush underneath her thermals and the impression of nipples poking through her vest. Then there was the holiday brochures with busty bikini clad babes all over the place and God bless the Sunday World; your weekly guarantee of flesh! Out of mass, into the newsagents, home for a wank! And lest we forget, the groundbreaking H&E; which somehow slipped under the sleaze radar as a 'Healthy lifestyle' magazine; the greatest cover for buying a jazz mag that was ever invented. "Oh, I'm a naturist meself" and off ya went guilt free to perv over nudists playing volleyball in all their hairy glory!

There are lapdancing clubs all over the country now, sure even Stringfellas came to Dublin. For a tenner ya can have a gorgeous girls arse stuck right in yer face, so close you can see her rusty sheriff's badge. Back in the old days it was challenge to figure out where to go to catch a glimpse of flesh that wasn't buried beneath layers of jumpers, skirts and wellies. The swimming pool certainly threw up many perving

possibilities, but it was all too risky. Swimming trunks and over anxious hormones could leave you stuck in the deep end until closing, when you were marched out wrinkled from head to toe with a woodie that wouldn't wane. The circus was a much less embarrassing proposition, it was the perfect cover for a bit of perving, as there would always be a couple of exotic foreign girls doing the trapeze or cracking a whip straddled on the back of pony, with nothing more than a top hat and a spangly leotard and legs that went all the way up to Heaven. Ohhhh, and flexible wasn't in it!

Sex shops are now as common as the local butchers once were. They are dens of sleaze, from videos and magazines to stuff that ya can shove up your arse. Sure, ya can buy a life size RealDoll* that is just like a real woman without the nagging. She'll cost ya thirty grand but ya can do what you want with her. We're looking for a second hand one on Ebay! Before the Naughties though, there were no sex toys or silicone women, you had to make do with the old soldiers' comfort** or a sheep that you were on a first name basis with. And the closest thing that women in those days could get to a vibrator was riding her bike down the bumpiest hill in the village.

Television in the 2000's is a virtual porn fest, with a million channels pumping out sleaze 24/7. There's Babecasts where ya can text and talk to four girls arses at the same time. Suburban Housewives stripping off in their semi- detached porn dens. If you want to see an enormous busted woman stick popcorn seeds up her arse, sit on a radiator, until they pop out and eat the whole lot, you'll undoubtedly find it on channel 69. Fair play to ya Rupert Murdoch, you're a pioneer.

But again, we find ourselves harking back to the days of using your imagination; wondering if Derek Davis and Thelma Mansfield ever did it during the ad breaks on Live at Three, picturing Anne Doyle naked from the waist down as she

*   Available from RealDoll.com
**   A jar of liver, that ya could cuddle up with and imagine was Sophia Loren's Italian love mound.

read the news, Bibi Baskin and how she might spank ya, and 'What in the World' ya could do with Teresa Lowe on a weekend away in Amsterdam.

CONCLUSION

So was Ireland better when no one talked about sex and it was nigh on impossible to get any in this country, unless you got married or you were a Bishop? Or are we better off with sex out the open* with all kinds of fetish clubs and swingers associations popping up in every housing estate in Ireland?

It's up to you dear reader to follow your own dirty path to find what batters your sausage or stirs your broth. Yes, you can buy your every filthy whim, you can be turned on by your phone, your telly, your computer or your silicone babe, but if ya ask me, and I'll take it that ya did, the biggest thrill is still from the perv that doesn't cost ya a penny; the illicit glimpse, the sneaky peek or whenever ya get a chance; the hole in the pocket brush off.

And don't worry there's still many a chance for a free perv in modern Ireland; ya just got to know where to look.

On the telly, for instance there are still plenty of lusty lasses to fantasize over; The Afternoon show with busty Blathnaid and the other one; two girls who undoubtedly know what to do with ya and how to do it, setting trembles off in thousands of pensioners' legs with their saucy make-up and wanton cleavage. Then there's the weather bitches talking right at ya, undressing you with their bedroom eyes and using meteorological double entendres like "warm front", "force ten" and "coming up from the South." Many dirty dreams are filled with travel totty Kathryn Thomas, fashion minxes Pamela Flood and Caroline Morahan and the ultimate male fantasy a Seoige sandwich.

If you're the sporting type why not go down to the gym and suspend yourself from the ceiling on a steel cable pulley system and drool over the Pilates class from your birds eye view. A sea of bouncing knockers and sweaty leotards!

Or get that seat at the bottom of the staircase on a double-decker bus and while away the hours watching ladies go up and down, praying for that one glimpse of knicker winking out at ya!

But if none of that does it for ya, you can always fork out some of your hard earned and go straight to the professionals.

Y'see, at the end of the day; that's what sex in modern Ireland is all about. Choice.

You can still have the thrill of the sneaky rub like in the old days, or ya can be a modern sexmonger and put your money where her mouth is. Nowadays, ya see, we Irish can have it both ways!

In fact, you can have it a number of ways. Depends on how open minded your partner is or how much cash you're willing to spend!

---

* *For anyone interested, Thursdays at 9pm. Quick Value car park, Ballydung Dogging Society meeting.*

A HISTORY OF CENS

AD
561
The only flesh permitted by the Church to be unclothed were the hands and face. Knees were only permitted airing on the longest day of Summer.

1010
Sex with animals was temporarily banned by the government. But reintroduced in 1941.

1503
Playing with yerself was banned outright by the Pope.

1607
Looking at a woman other than your wife was declared a mortal sin.

1839
Any citizen caught masturbating over any image of Queen Victoria would be executed.

1931
Confessions of an illicit carnal nature had to be repeated slowly, twice to your priest.

1947
Swimming in the ocean was only permitted for men whilst wearing a knitted Aran wet suit. Many drowned with the feckin' weight of the things.

1952
Flakes were banned from the popular ice cream cone; the 99 as they were deemed too provocative.

1964
If actors and actress were to have a 'relationship' on television or stage, they had to be married in real life.

1965
Bishop Carney of Donegal, stated that no mixed cars were allowed on the bumper cars in Bundoran. Other seaside parishes were quick to follow.

1969
Magazines mentioning ladies sanitary products were described as 'filthy dirty' by the Legion of Mary and banned outright.

ORSHIP IN IRELAND

1970
Aer Lingus hostesses were asked not to handle sausages on board any flights for risk of causing in-flight erections, which may in turn cause an obstruction during an emergency landing. The practice of covering cooked breakfasts with tin foil remains to this day.

1986
The Thatch pub in Dunfarten was burnt to the ground after the owner Ted Drew refused to remove a cardboard Sam Fox backed peanut display, before the final two bags of peanuts were sold. The local priest Father Nerney refused to condemn the arson attack, saying, "He might as well get used to fire, as he's going to hell anyway."

1988
The parish of Peddlers Rag decreed that couples courting in cars had to have two bags of turf in the back seat at all times.

1989
Page Three model Linda Lusardi is refused entry at Dublin airport when she arrived to appear for the opening of 'The Thatch 2' in Dunfarten.

1990
Cartoon characters on RTE had to be wearing clothes, or the programme could not be aired. The Pink Panther was not seen on Irish screens until 1993.

1992
The first official top shelf magazine reached our shores on Friday June 17th. 'Playboy' was finally available in your local newsagent. Absenteeism from the workplace on the following Monday was up to 68%.

1995
Mary Gilhooley, from Cabra, Dublin, is the first Irish woman to purchase a vibrator from Ireland's first porn shop 'House of Wank.' However Mary (23) claimed it was for her rheumatism.

1996
With the advent of a new thing called the Internet this was the year that no one really gave a shite anymore!

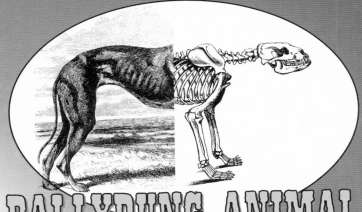

BALLYDUNG ANIMAL RENDERING CENTRE

**Bring us your sick or unwanted animals and pets and we'll take care of the dirty deed.
With prices to die for!**

FREE TOURS
of the facility!
Tour includes:
The Killing Rooms,
The Pelt Stripper,
The Gutting Tables,
The Incinerator,
The Glue Making Sheds.
And kids can kill a budgie!

SPECIAL THIS MONTH:
Your pet's paw on a keyring - €9.95
or two paws for €15!

Price list:
Horse - €20
Dog - €12
Cat - €10
Kittens - €2 each.

Directions:
3rd left from Ballydung off the R706,
towards the caves, then follow the smell!

Schedule

7 – 9am MILK THE COWS
with Matt Mongey.
Featuring Mickey and Willy the Leprechauns. With their helium style funny voices and risqué humour, who knows who or what they'll make fun of this week?

9 – 11am WOMEN'S THINGS
with Una Brow.
Contact Una on the Brow-line with your comments and opinions.

11am – 2pm LIGHT LUNCH
with LIAM.
Innocuous chatter and eighties ballads galore with Liam. And don't forget you can win a prize if you can guess what's in LIAM'S LUNCHBOX?

2 – 4pm AFTERNOON DELIGHT
with DJ Vince Fahey.
Sure ya never know what Vince will play next? DEATH NOTICES at 3pm and HELP ME WITH ME HOMEWORK at 3.30pm

4 – 7pm NUN ON THE RUN
with Sister Flikka.
Ballydung's No.1 Nun playing only No.1's. Please note that during Lent Sister Flikka will be taking a vow of silence. But that only means more No.1's to drive ya home!

7 – 8pm FADO FADO
with Tommy Squitters.
An hour of reminiscing and the odd tall tale with the memory man himself.

8 – 10pm BLOW IT OUT YER RADIO
with Ballydung's very own fellas off the telly DJ Podge and DJ Rodge.
With, chat, craic, mart results, weather and music. Live sessions from such artists as Murt the Bulge Winfrey, Lesbian Sandwich, Ambrose McAuley the singing surgeon, The Pubes and Dead Kitten Society.

10 – Midnight
with THE PSYCHIC DYKE
hosted by Miss Sprinkles and her psychic dog Bytch, Irelands only Tarot reading canine.

Midnight – 7am NIGHT STROKES
with DJ Andy Whank.
Keeping ya company through the night with mellow sounds, shipping forecast and radio bingo. And on the hour the ever popular GUESS THE NOISE?

Sputum's Travel

Arse Street, Ballydung, Co.Ring.
Telephone: 316 Fax: 317

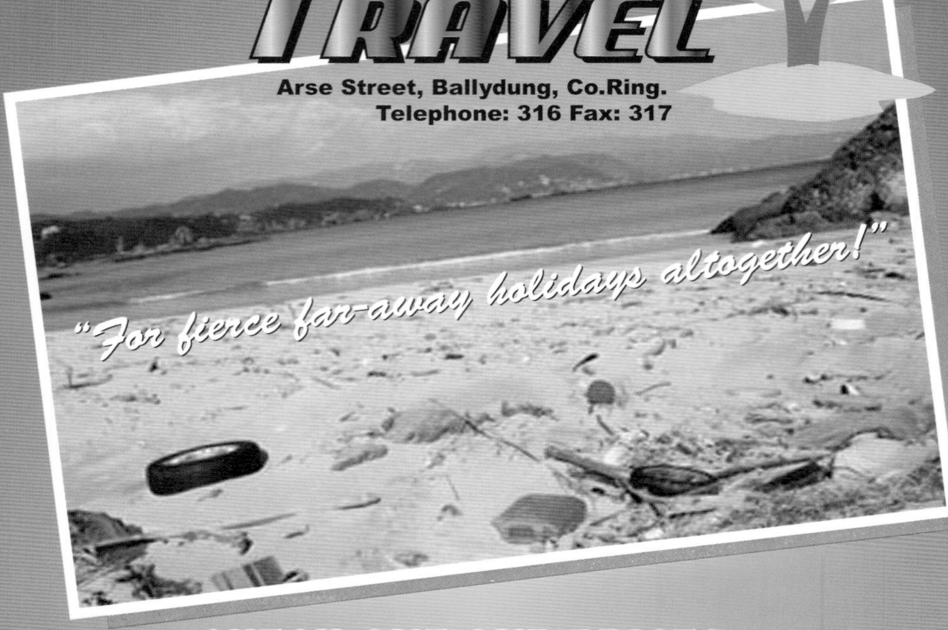

"For fierce far-away holidays altogether!"

CHECK OUT OUR PRICES:

★ **Bundoran**   **6 nights B/B**
€106 pp

★ **Isle Of Man**   **1 week H/B**
€236 pp

★ **Beirut**   **1 week H/B**
€106 pp   **(Including Flak Jacket)**

★ **Gaza Strip**   **3 nights**
€169 pp   **2 ★ hotel**
          (Ideal Stag location)

**Visit the
LAS VEGAS
of the south-east
TRAMORE**

**Long
Cocky**

**Honey
Moons**

Lourdes

BROWN'S STARS

WITH LARRY BROWN - PSYCHIC AND COBBLER

★ ★

AQUARIUS
The Water Carrier
(21 Jan- 18 Feb)
Typically, Aquarians have misshapen genitals. Mothers deliberately try to avoid having babies under this sign. And as your ruling planet is Uranus let's face it, you don't stand a chance.

TAURUS
The Bull
(21 Apr - 21 May)
Ah, Taurus. You've done your best to live a good life. Yet, things are still shite. Unfortunately, they won't get any better. My advice is take to the bottle, then take to your bed. No one will notice you're missing anyway.

LEO
The Lion
(23 Jul - 23 Aug)
With the Sun as your ruling planet, you are supposed to be passionate, fiery and courageous. What a shame no one likes you enough to ever find out if any of this shite is true about you.

SCORPIO
The Scorpion
(24 Oct - 22 Nov)
You're gay. Everyone knows it and you're fooling no one. Stop pretending it isn't true, leave the rest of us decent folk alone and go sign up for Mardi Gras.

PISCES
The Two Fishes
(20 Feb - 20 Mar)
Things haven't been going well for you in recent times. Well, sorry to have to tell you this, but there's worse to come. For your own sake, stay away from traffic and don't eat seafood when there's a 'd' in the day.

GEMINI
The Twins
(22 May - 21 Jun)
Geminis are changeable by nature. I call that two faced. Is it any wonder no one returns your calls? You should be glad you're a duel sign as it's the only relationship you'll ever be part of.

VIRGO
The Virgin
(24 Aug - 22 Sep)
Virgos are repellent to the opposite sex. There are a very few exceptions to this rule but you are not one of them. That is why people always laugh when they hear you are the Virgin sign. Because it's clear to everyone you are one.

SAGITTARIUS
The Centaur
(23 Nov - 21 Dec)
Sagittarians consider themselves to be entrepreneurial. That's not the same thing as being a scabby prick. You never get a round in, swap price tags in shops and were still stealing from your mother's purse at 23.

ARIES
The Ram
(21 Mar - 20 Apr)
Your ruling planet Mars has it in for you this week. Don't leave the house. In fact…if I'm honest, it's going to get you sooner or later so you may as well know you won't be enjoying a long life.

CANCER
The Crab
(22 Jun - 22 Jul)
Did you know, that statistically Cancereans are 95% more likely than any other sign to have crabs? Don't be surprised if people run a mile when they hear what sign you are.

LIBRA
The Scales
(23 Sep - 23 Oct)
Librans are supposedly charming, kind and gentle natured. So what the hell happened to you, you cold hearted bastard?

CAPRICORN
The Goat
(22 Dec - 20 Jan)
Your friends and family won't tell you this because they feel sorry for you, but everyone thinks it's hilarious that you were born a Capricorn, as you really do have a head like a goat.

PODGE AND RODGE EXPOSED

uncommonly violent end. Once they had disposed of the body of their grandfather Helmut Thomas O Leprosy, they wasted no time in pawning off his war medals and leather shoes. They raised fourteen shillings and six pence. Their grandfather's life was worth a bicycle, a bag of bullseyes and two sucky pops *and a catapult* to these demented six year olds. It was the last straw when their mother Hooreen discovered her father in law's corpse stuffed under the Aga. The boys had to go ~~X~~ to School!

The books at Ballydung ~~Asylum~~ *National School* record the dates of entry of Podraig and Rodraig as the 11th of May 1948. Which was also the last day that the two were to ever see their mother again.

Professor Murdoch, who trained at the Vienna Institute of the Insane , psychologically assessed the twins and the diagnosis was startling. They were both suffering from Gooburger Syndrome which meant that as individuals they were bad, but together they were literally pure evil. Immediate treatment was instigated and despite the emotional distress for the two siblings, it was deemed necessary that they be kept apart and live in separate wings of the asylum building. During this separation period, which lasted over a year, little progress was made with Rodge, who couldn t integrate and chose to play with himself (something that became an even bigger problem in later years!) Podge on the other hand seemed to thrive and read extensively from the asylum's library. At the age of seven, Podge challenged Professor Murdoch's diagnosis in front of the board of management and not only that, exposed Murdoch's addiction to nitrous oxide (laughing gas). Murdoch left the establishment in disgrace, however he returned five years later as a patient.

ALL UTTER SHITE !!!

For a seven year old to display such a highly
intelligent but devious mind was worrying, but back
in the day Podge managed to come across as cute .
With Murdoch gone, it wasn't long until Podge
manipulated the staff into making his and his
brother's life as comfortable as possible. They were
soon back together and had a room of their own. It
was here in the asylum that the O Leprosy brothers
truly felt at home.

(good!)

IF YOU PRINT THIS MINGUS WE'LL CUT YOUR HEAD OFF AND SHIT DOWN YOUR NECK!

They were cared for by a psychiatric nurse whom
they called Granny. She was in fact one of the
inmates who liked to impersonate members of the
staff. It is here with the clinically insane and
warped minds of the ~~asylum inmates~~ *teachers* that Podge and
Rodge got their education.

The only father figure that the boys ever had
during their formative years was the groundskeeper
Michael Scratcher or The Captain* as he was known,
who was Granny s male companion on and off for   ** FUCKIN LEGEND!*
twenty years or so. The Captain would satisfy his
incredibly violent temperament by disappearing for
months on end, to all corners of the world as a
hired mercenary. Podge and Rodge looked up to the
Captain and they loved hearing his tales of blood
and guts and adventure. This is where Podge, in
particular, got his inspiration for gruesome story
telling and Rodge revelled in the Captain s stories
of the naughty things that ladies in foreign lands
would do to ya. **HOW DARE YOU ANALYSE ME YOU PRICK!!**

As you can tell, The Captain was a very influential
figure during these formative years and would remain
so until the early sixties when he failed to return
after a holiday in Vietnam.

Podge's Diary

Jaysus, this country is shite. 37 years old and still not getting any? What the feck is wrong with women these days? I brushed off Gussie Bollokin's left one last night after the bingo and thought I was in with a chance until she kneed me in the bollix. And she'd been teasing me all night with her tiny skirt that showed her knees when she sat down. I've been reading recently in a foreign newspaper about a kind of woman called a lesbian, girls who like other girls. That sounded great to me until I realised it's just the girls they like — no fellas at all! Anyway, after the shite luck I've been having over the last, well over me whole life, I'm convinced the women of Ballydung have caught this lesbian disease. It might be in the water. Having a gobshite of a brother like Rodge doesn't help. I make a bit of an effort, but it's like not realising you've stepped in shite the smell follows you around and puts people off. He's a real thorn in me side the useless little prick. I'd hoped he wouldn't live this long what with all the diseases he's had over the last thirty years, but he's like a feckin' cockroach.

On the plus side, I got me first customer for me new human taxidermy service today. Some fella's booked in his Auntie to be stuffed. Apparently she was a real geebag and now that she's dead, the family want her stuffed and are going to use her as a scarecrow. With a bit of luck, me business will start taking off if I make a good job of this one. The only problem is, I'm not quite sure what I'm doing, but I'll just hollow her out and take it from there. How hard can it be?

Have to go now, as Rodge has just come home saying he's been sacked from the abbatoir again. Hope the little bastard at least grabbed a side of beef on the way out.

Podge

Note for the day: Idi Amin ousted. What a shame.

FORGOTTEN IRELAND

PART 1

Things ya don't even know ya miss!

POUFFES: No living room was complete without a couple of pouffes to park yer tired feet or yer lazy arse on. Fantastic for tripping over in the dark.

DOG SHIT ON THE PAVEMENT: The hilarity of you and your friends walking down the pavement and one of yis sliding in a big pile of steaming dog turd.

WHITE DOG POO : Ya just don't see it anymore do ya? And why was it white? Nobody ever knew the secret of the white poo!

SONAS: Couldn't understand a feckin' word of it, but you looked like an eejit or a cheapskate if ya didn't have a copy in school.

THE A-SIDE AND THE B-SIDE: Ah records. Mind you, ya don't have to get up mid-shag anymore to turn them over!

STRING ART: The art of winding coloured bits of string in a pattern around hundreds of nails in a block of chipboard. And thinking you were Salvador 'feckin' Dali once you'd done it!

CHILDREN WITH MANNERS: Gone are the days when children knew their place and wouldn't call any adult ' ya fat bastard'

BUBBLEGUM CARDS: When ya could get pictures from your favourite filum and a hard slab of pink gum, that would disintegrate into a milky chemical and horse hoof soup in yer mouth.

PLASTIC BAGS IN THE HEDGEROWS:

The drunk drivers beacon on many a country hedge. Guiding ya home, when ya could hardly see the road and certainly weren't sober enough to read a sign.

GOLLY BAR: Vanilla ice cream with a hint of racism.

BIG STEREO SPEAKERS: Whether in yer house or in yer car, the bigger the speakers the cooler ya were!

FORTYCOATS: Bizarrre children's TV character who ran a flying sweetshop! Far too dodgy for children's television nowadays!

SHIT JOKES WE FOUND FUNNY IN THE '80s

HOW LONG DID LIONEL RICHIE SIT ON THE TOILET?
ALL NIGHT LONG!!

WHAT DO YOU CALL PAC-MAN ON DRUGS?
CRACK MAN!!

WHY SHOULD YOU NEVER FLY WITH BA?
COS HE AIN T GETTIN ON NO PLANE FOOL!

WHAT KIND OF WOOD DOESN T FLOAT?
NATALIE WOOD!

WHAT DO YOU GET IF YOU CROSS A ROBOT
WITH A PIRATE?
ARRRRRRGH 2D2.

WHAT'S THE FIRST SIGN OF MADNESS?
SUGGS WALKING UP YOUR DRIVEWAY.

WHAT DID THE MUMMY BUFFALO SAY TO HER
CHILD AS HE LEFT FOR SCHOOL?
BISON.

HOW MANY LETTERS ARE IN THE ALPHABET?
22 – COS ET WENT HOME AND SOMEBODY SHOT JR!

WHAT IS THE MOST DIFFICULT PART OF ROLLERBLADING?
TELLING YOUR PARENTS YOU'RE GAY

A 10 00 PM CURFEW WAS IMPOSED IN BELFAST. EVERYBODY
HAD TO BE OFF THE STREETS OR RISK BEING SHOT.
HOWEVER ONE CITIZEN WAS SHOT AT 9 45PM.
"WHY DID YOU DO THAT?" THE SOLDIER WAS ASKED BY HIS
SUPERIOR OFFICER.
"I KNOW WHERE HE LIVES" HE REPLIED "AND HE WOULDN'T
HAVE MADE IT".

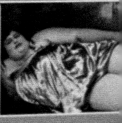

WASH DOWN YER WELLIES, IT'S THAT TIME OF YEAR AGAIN!

THE BALLYDUNG BACHELOR FESTIVAL NOW ON!

FIND LOVE, ROMANCE AND BALLYDUNG'S ONLY €9.99 BUFFET!

The week long festival features such events as:
- 'Lady lifting competition – gentlemen, how many ladies can you lift?

- Blindfold ploughing competition.

- Fester 'n' Ailin's Cross Dressing Ball.

- Who'll take a bath? competition.

- Speed dating and dancing.

- Nude inter-county hurling.

- Back again due to popular demand 'Guess the colour of the ladies' knickers?'

All bachelors and single ladies welcome! Sure ya never know who you'll meet at the BALLYDUNG BACHELOR FESTIVAL!

Ladies FREE

Gentlemen €50 (Redheads €60) Registration fee.

```Rooms available by the hour, contact Margo, Casa Margo Ballydung 777-243.

## TRACTOR PARKING AVAILABLE.

```

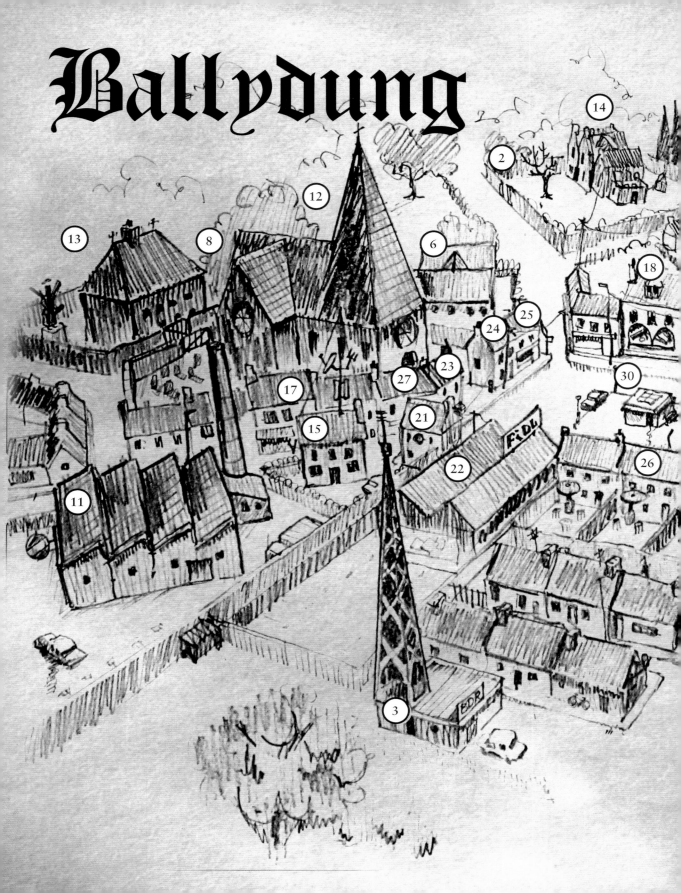

Ballydung

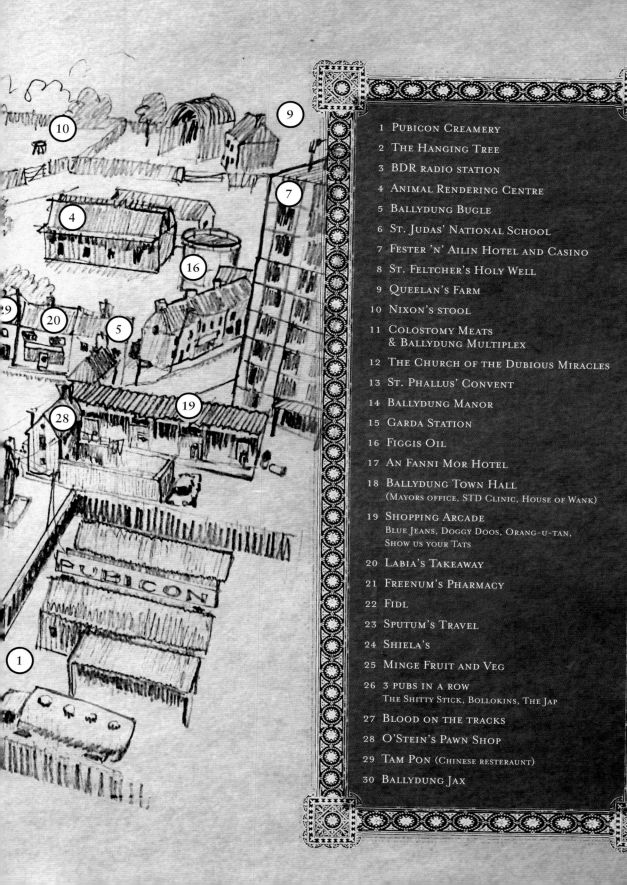

1 Pubicon Creamery

2 The Hanging Tree

3 BDR radio station

4 Animal Rendering Centre

5 Ballydung Bugle

6 St. Judas' National School

7 Fester 'n' Ailin Hotel and Casino

8 St. Feltcher's Holy Well

9 Queelan's Farm

10 Nixon's stool

11 Colostomy Meats
& Ballydung Multiplex

12 The Church of the Dubious Miracles

13 St. Phallus' Convent

14 Ballydung Manor

15 Garda Station

16 Figgis Oil

17 An Fanni Mor Hotel

18 Ballydung Town Hall
(Mayors office, STD Clinic, House of Wank)

19 Shopping Arcade
Blue Jeans, Doggy Doos, Orang-u-tan,
Show us your Tats

20 Labia's Takeaway

21 Freenum's Pharmacy

22 Fidl

23 Sputum's Travel

24 Shiela's

25 Minge Fruit and Veg

26 3 pubs in a row
The Shitty Stick, Bollokins, The Jap

27 Blood on the tracks

28 O'Stein's Pawn Shop

29 Tam Pon (Chinese resteraunt)

30 Ballydung Jax

SINGLE FELLA'S PAGE

Podge's Diary

December 19th 1983

Can't believe it's nearly 1984. I've done feck all with the 1980's so far, although at least it means my 5 year ban on operating a taxidermy service is nearly up. I'm going to start off doing animals for a while this time, until I get the hang of it.

I wonder when 1984 comes around will it be like that famous book? The one about being watched all the time, and everyone being paranoid....what was it called? The Moving Finger that was it.

I asked Margo Minge from down the town out today. But the cow said she was already stepping out with someone — some ponce who wears them new 'runner boots' and has a cassette walkman. He's from some big town like Tubbercurry or somewhere. Prick. So I got Rodge to put a brick through her front window. I'm already over it. A foreign woman moved into the town last weekend — I think she's from Poland or Germany or somewhere. She's a big eastern block of a woman with a glint in her eye, so I reckon if I get in there first, she won't know any better.

I'm doing me usual Christmas charity raffle again this year. Going to say it's for the black babies, as that particular cause is gettin' fierce trendy altogether at the moment. I'm planning to use the money to buy a telly. I usually make a good few quid so I might even be able to afford one of them fancy coloured ones. Typical though — I finally get a telly and M*A*S*H is axed. Now I'll never know what all the fuss was about.

Have to go. Me and waste-of-space Rodge are getting the bus to see Flashdance at the Ballydung Screen. Apparently there's more than a glimpse of nipple in it!

Podge

FORGOTTEN IRELAND
PART 2

Things ya don't even know ya miss!

THE KERRYMAN JOKE: An entire county and its inhabitants being the butt of everyone's joke!

BUBBLEGUM CIGARS: Just like the real thing, but bubble gum flavoured.

CANDY CIGARETTES: A box of milky candy fags, to set ya on the way to a forty a day habit.

SPUD GUNS: Guns that actually fired pellets of hard potato. Would take an eye out at twenty paces.

JANE FONDA WORKOUT VIDEOS: A totally different workout depending on whether you are a middle-aged housewife or a pubescent teenage boy.

METAL ICE CUBE TRAYS: The only way to make ice cubes back in the day. So cold that they'd freezer burn the fingerprints right off your fingers.

MONBACKS: The fellas up in Dublin who'd back you into a car space saying 'C'mon back'. Always dressed in an official cap stolen from a bus conductor and a rolled up newspaper. And if ya didn't tip them, they'd key yer car!

WASSUP: Feckin' gobshites reciting 'wassup' from a beer ad that got annoying after the first viewing.

SPANGLES: Fizzy fruity squares with a dimple in the middle! Sucky delight!

'A WEAR' FOR MEN : They just stopped caring for men and their fashion needs when they closed down.

SODASTREAM: A highly explosive gas cylinder for kids to play with and carbonate just about anything, including the family pet. Make yourself any flavour of fizzy drink with an array of syrup flavouring so full of E-numbers you'd have a headache for week!

CALCULATOR WATCH: With more buttons than the Starship Enterprise; you could read the time and add shit up.

THE BREAD VAN: Back in the day they'd bring the bread to you. There was hardly anything more fun than stoning the bread van!

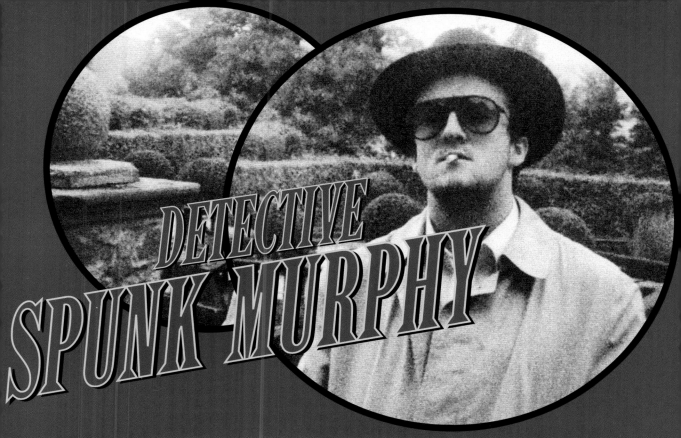

PRIVATE DICK FOR HIRE

Formerly of Limerick CID, Ex - Guantanamo Processing Centre

20 years experience in the world of Investigation. Authorised weapons carrier. Fluent in Ghurkha and Swahili.

YOU WANT TO KNOW THE ANSWERS; I'M THE ANSWER MAN!

From Infidelity, Adultery, Missing Persons, Background checks, Pilferage, Theft, Surveillance, Missing Pets, Relationships with Pets, Ghosts, Revenge, Addiction, DNA retrieval, Repo, Honey Traps

"I'VE SEEN IT ALL, I'VE SOLVED IT ALL. WITH MY TRACK RECORD OF 100%
I will sort out any problem guaranteed or your money back!"*

IF YOU WANT A HAPPY ENDING OR JUST AN ENDING - GET YOUR HANDS ON SPUNK!

CALL: 1885 SPUNK

*Less expenses and non-repayable up front payment.

HOW TO SPOT A GAY

HOW TO SPOT A GAY

USING THE GAYDAR:
These colours correspond to the various levels of Gay.
Green = mildly faggy,
Yellow = dangerous benny tendencies
Orange =Well on the brown road to gay
Pink = Rampant homo

Tear this useful sheet out and keep it with you at all times, if a fella you know scores over five greens, four yellows, two oranges and any pink at all, it's time to keep your back to the wall! There's a benny on the loose!

HOW TO SPOT A GAY
There are many ways to spot the wily gay in your midst. The gay for one reason or another sometimes prefers to remain anonymous. Here's all you'll ever need to know about how to spot a gender bender from fifty yards.

Read the signs: know your man
A man who wear sandals.
He likes to cook.
If he's been to the theatre more than twice in one year.
If he can recommend a 'good dry white wine'
A man that lines toilet paper on the seat before taking a dump.
He prefers to go to a hairdressers instead of a barbers.
He prefers 'Desperate Housewives' to '24.'
There are five urinals; the first and last one are occupied, if he uses any one other than number three (the middle one)
If he can answer the question "who won the first Big Brother?"
Any pubic topiary or actually knowing the word 'Manscapping'
Men who use moisturiser.
Men who use moisturiser with a hint of tan.
He eats sushi more than once.
He enjoys house make-over shows.
Owns more than three pairs of shoes (excluding trainers)
Asks you if his 'bum looks big in this?'
Owns a Nissan Figaro
Walks around in his bare feet in the office
Owns a very small dog or an enormous dog.
Rings his mates, just for a chat.
Knowing star signs and the dates they fall under
Knowing the symbols that star signs represent
Doesn't follow a football team (soccer or GAA)
He plays rugby
He thinks lap dancing is 'degrading to women'
Drinks skimmed milk
Knows how to do any ballroom dance
Enjoys French films including the ones with no nudity
Is afraid of monkeys

BALLYDUNG
IR 246022
26 SEP 69

HOOREEN O'LEPROSY
(NEE GAWKIN)

IRELAND'S
TOP TOTTY

As vetted by Podge & Rodge

20 Twink
A legend of Irish stage and screen, the blonde bomshell, with legs that go all the way to Heaven. We get a Maxi Dick every time we see Twink strutting her stuff!

19 Katy French
This Frenchie is less garlic and onions, more bra and panties! The lingerie queen, who was once famously dumped by her waiter boyfriend for being far too spicy a dish! We'd like seconds please!

18 Caroline Morahan & Pamela Flood
Fashion gurus and sex goddesses! When they come on our screens so do we! With Carloline's lips and bra busting boobs, and Pamela's leggy legginess, they're every Irishman's three in a bed fantasy!

17 Lucy Kennedy
Juicy Lucy. The juicy bit because she is the colour of an orange. With the dirtiest laugh on telly and a naughty glint in her eye, and if she can handle us, she'll handle yours!

16 Toni the Exotic Dancer
Ireland's only exotic dancer in the eighties, with boobs so big they needed a separate van each to get them around. Like Funderland in an RDS sized bra. She'll always hold a special place in Irish men's pants!

15 Margo
She sings the Holy songs, but there's a divil inside her. She's strict and she'd rule ya in the bedroom but she'd make ya a lovely cup of tea and a slice of apple tart afterwards.

14 Miriam O'Callaghan
This Amazon woman lights up our screens. She can talk the talk with the country's politicians. She's strict, sexy and seven foot tall. And we've been very naughty boys!

13 Grainne & Sile Seoige
The Sexiest Sisters since The Nolans. Dark and pouty, these Galway siblings are so sexy that RTE have to put out a public health warning whenever the two appear on the screen at the same time!

12 Glenda Gilson
Ireland's only model, strutting her sexy swimsuit bod, making those tabloid rags worth buying. She hasn't got 'come to bed' eyes, she's got 'come to bed eyebrows!' 9.5 on the wrister scale!

11 Blathnaid Ní Chofaigh

The red-on-the-head, good-in-the-bed girl herself! The only reason to watch television in the afternoon (with your pants down of course!)

10 Amanda Brunker

Former Miss Ireland, current sexpot! With a cleavage that's like looking down the port tunnel and a saucy sexy voice, that'd whisper dirty nothings in yer ear! Brunkers bunker, is one we wouldn't mind getting stuck in!

9 Mary Black

Dark and sultry Irish songbird. With eyes that would melt yer heart and a voice that would give ya the horn! Still one of our fantasy favourites!

8 Kathryn Thomas

There's nothing better than watching a fine young thing travelling around the world in tight t-shirts and bikinis looking out through yer telly, with a 'wish you were here' twinkle in her eye! Don't worry Kathryn, we're coming!

7 Mary McEvoy

Ah, Biddy, we'll never forget ya. Well, Holy God; to see her traipsing around Glenroe in her wellies on a Sunday evening would set our hearts a-fluttering and our pants a-tightening! She made Sundays very unholy for many a man!

6 Anna Nolan

Outside of lads' magazines, most lezzers look like fellas. But not our Anna! She keeps Irish men's lesbian fantasies alive and we'd certainly like to try and get her back on the meat.

5 Sinead O'Connor

Bald and mad as a brush. But jaysus, eyes like a doe and the voice of an angel. Spit on me Sinead!!

4 Anne Doyle

She's given us good and bad news over the years, but we've never listened to a word of it. Those secret smiles tell us that below that news desk, she's wearing nothing but a tan, and we know Doyler would know a trick or two.

3 Rosanna Davison

Dull as hell, but we still wouldn't mind this 'lady in bed'! She was officially the best looking girl in the world a few years back - not the kind you'd marry though - de Burgh as a father in law? Next!

2 Nadine Coyle

We bet she's glad she was dumped from Six! As are we, 'cos if she'd made it, she'd be working in Supermacs now rather than showing off her lovely thighs in micro minis. We don't understand a word she says, but that only makes her more lovely.

1 The Corrs

They've been on the go for years, but we still can't decide which one we'd do first. A problem we're sure Jim can relate to!

I LOVE YOU!

GAYS' MAZE

MEN WORKING

Alan Hughes

Manicure Stop

Tanning Stop

Brian Kennedy

Visit Mark from Westlife

Public Toilet Stop

Graham Norton

UNCLAIMED ITEMS
BLOWOUT SALE NOW ON!

O'STEIN'S PAWN SHOP
BALLYDUNG SQUARE

We're clearing the shelves! No reasonable offer refused!

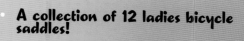

- A collection of 12 ladies bicycle saddles!

- Prosthetic leg - toes all same length so could be used for either leg.

- Dead monkey - was alive when pawned. Half price this week only.

- Radio/ Cassette Ghetto Blaster - with bass button. Radio broken. Single cassette deck.

- Multi speed Travel Vag – high speed not working, needs proper cleaning.

- Heated toilet seats from Japan.

- Set of matching coffee & tea jars.

- Guide Dog.

- David Essex LP's (5 of).

- P Diddy punchbag.

- Eye of toad, tail of newt.

- Collection of varnished frogs.

- Chalk.

- "What The Butler Saw" amusement machine.

- A rusty sheriff's badge.

- Gerry Ryan autographed handkerchief.

- Left handed hammer.

- Left handed screwdriver.

- Left handed saw.

- Electric guitar and cord.

- Box of VHS tapes including: Convoy, The Russians are Coming, Spies Like Us, The Thing,

- The Lovers Guide 1&2.

Please note we are not accepting any more 'Travel with Hector' Books.

THE STATE OF THE NATION

CHAPTER 4: HOLIDAYS

"Tropical diseases will give ya coughs and wheezes, a swollen sack, a lump on yer back, there's symptoms many more." Fester & Ailin.

Lyrics taken from the No.1 single 'Tropical Diseases' from the 1975 album 'Down the Furry Glen' available on Shitehawk records, Mullingar. Lyrics reprinted by kind permission of Mick Fester and Tony Ailin.

INTRODUCTION

The first recorded holiday in Ireland was 'The Flight of the Earls' in 1607 when a bunch of Earl fellas went on a package holiday to Spain and never came back*. Despite what the history books say they went by boat not by air.

Holidaying nowadays is big business, with travel companies doing deals left right and centre, never has it been cheaper in Irish history to go anywhere ya feckin' want than it is now. But it wasn't always that way. The history of the Irish and holidaying is littered with sunburnt corpses, rashes on your mickey and bad swimsuit decisions.

There is plenty of evidence to support the theory that our ancestors used to go on holidays, even back as far as the Stoneage. Primitive ice cream cones made from hollowed out Leprechaun skulls, and deer skin speedos were found at Newgrange. Many carved stone buckets and spades have been found sprinkled along the coastline of Ireland. The corpses of a Neolithic family were found under what appears to be a windbreaker made of stone, which by all accounts crushed them, more than likely, after a freak breeze caught them by surprise.

"I shall sit in a field and it shall be my refuge for a dozen days or more." Mossy Stools, poet, author, chancer (1756-1810)

The most popular holiday for many centuries in Ireland was 'Sitting in a Field.' It was cheap, relaxing and occasionally fun. Only men were allowed to go on holidays back then; a

rule that the fellas made up 'cause they wanted a rest from the nagging wives and the fifteen brats.

"I'm off on a holiday," our ancestor would say, and with a pipe in his mouth and a few bottles of whiskey, the Irish male would set off to find a suitable field to sit in for a week or so.

It was all grand until one summer a lad brought a chair with him into the field. Naturally everyone thought he had ideas above his station, and from that day on, what you sat on in the field became a sort of status symbol. The better the seat ya sat on, coupled with the duration of your stay in the field, showed the rest of your village how important ya were, without you having to say so. It was the ultimate 'mickey swinging' of its day.

The simple act of 'sitting in a field' soon became ridiculously competitive. It was no longer a holiday, the Irish male ego had transformed it into a challenge that would ultimately end in death!

As the summers went by, year after year fellas would attempt to outdo one another. Some lads used a whole year's earnings to import expensive fancy chairs from Japan or Morocco, just so they could sit on their holes in a field and feel better than everyone else.

It all came to a head in 1892 when Malachy McGooley of Fiddlersminge and Rusty McGee, originally from Smelme Passage ended up sitting in the same field. When neither would back down nor leave, a battle of wills ensued. The two

---

* *The fact they didn't return, doesn't quite qualify as a holiday, but shag that, it's my book and I can claim what I like! Now feck off back up there and keep reading ya gobshite!*

sat in their respective corners for over four months until Malachy keeled over dead from malnutrition and piles. Rusty, barely alive, and only surviving by eating bits of himself was heard to say, as they carried him out of the field, that it was the best holiday he had ever had. After that 'sitting in a field' lost its appeal as a holiday option in Ireland.

If the truth be told, no one dared to try and outdo Rusty McGee, who ironically could never sit in a field again even if he'd wanted to, as he had eaten his own arse* during that fateful Summer in 1892.

PACKAGE HELLADAY

Back in the day if you said, "I'm going on holiday" that meant you were going somewhere in Ireland. It was only if you said "I'm going abroad" that you were leaving the country and most likely going to Spain or Portugal. These were considered mad faraway places altogether.

In fact, it wasn't until the Fifties that the Irish dared leave the Emerald Isle and travel further than Tramore or Bettystown for what the Yanks like to call a 'vacation.'

Only fourteen people travelled abroad in the year 1952. These virgin travellers never returned due to death by sunburn and/or horrendous dysentery. It was obvious that no Irishman or woman could hack more than an hour of sun a day. The government banned holidays after the tragedy of the 'Torremolinos fourteen'. The ban was eventually lifted in the Sixties and the Irish could once more go abroad and get the legs burnt off them.

It would be fair to say that during the Sixties and Seventies we weren't the most sophisticated travellers. Wherever the Irish went, we brought everything and the kitchen sink with us. All Irish suitcases would have a man's belt tied around it for extra security, and a busted zipper was like a badge of honour. The compulsory green piece of wool was attached proudly to the handle, which was far more important than having a tag with your name on it. The case itself would be crammed with a number of essential items; jacks roll, a bottle of milk of magnesia, a box of teabags and sausages and rashers in case the food was muck. And most importantly a 'Big oul coat' for everybody just in case it wasn't as hot as the Travel Agent** had promised.

The Travel Agent, a once colourful character, is now thankfully almost extinct in modern Ireland. Right up to the new millennium you couldn't go anywhere without going through this gatekeeper to the world. His domain was filled with tanned young ones working on phones, maps of the world with coloured thumb tacks sprinkled across the seven continents denoting places that he or one of the girls (or he and one of the girls) had visited and thought were 'smashing places altogether.' And then there were the brochures. Ohhh, the brochures! Even if you weren't intending to go anywhere, the holiday brochures were the best free wank material available outside of the Damart catalogue. But the Travel Agent was a wily creature and it was nearly impossible to leave without signing up to go somewhere foreign. The amount of young horny men in the Seventies who went in to the Travel Agents to simply pick up a free jizz brochure and ended up spending half their year's wages on a week in Corfu is impossible to calculate.

Like the Seanachai of old, the Travel Agents were great tale spinners and storytellers. Everywhere they suggested was a paradise; constant sunshine, not too hot mind, the locals so friendly they'd let ya stay in their homes, and the girls were just like the ones in the brochure except even sexier. But they were lying bastards of the highest order and while your hard earned cash was sitting in their till, you, the unsuspecting traveller were setting off on a holiday to hell!

WISH YOU WEREN'T HERE!

Your two week relaxing break begins at the bank, where you end up in a queue. In front of you is a feckin' eejit with the breath of a beggar's anus, who jabbers on about all the great places he's been to, whilst behind you is a twisted ould geebag with emphysema who phlegms all over yer back. And when you finally get to the window, some hatchet faced wagon informs you that they have no Pesos left, and that you should have booked some months ago. Instead she gives you a bunch of travellers' cheques that can only be cashed in three hotels in Spain. And yours isn't one of them.

Then there's the charter flight that must leave at 3am and you've to check in nine hours beforehand. After queuing for a lifetime, the check-in desk closes and the grumpy cow says those immortal words, "I'm sorry, you'll have to join the other queue!"

The plane itself last saw action in Pearl Harbour, it barely makes it off the ground and you've got to face six hours breathing in recirculated farts, B.O. and cheese and onion crisps. The seats are so small that they were made by Fisher Price, and you're sandwiched between the fattest couple in Ireland, who insisted on changing into the same holiday clothing that they've been wearing since 1965. When they sit down 98% of the fabric disappears up their crevices. And with the slightest bit of turbulence, the sweaty fat mans scrotum manages to pop out and rub off your elbow. At this point deep vein thrombosis would be a welcome relief!

---

*   He said it tasted like 'dirty chicken.'
** The modern equivalent of the 'Travel Agent' is called the 'Internet' and despite not even being a real person can turn out to be as big a feckin' liar!

The ex-Soviet Union prison camp interrogators turned air hostesses throw you a tray of unidentifiable slop sealed in impregnable packaging. The packaging tastes better than the food. After four hours your kidneys start to seize up but you daren't ask the hostess for some water, as you get the unnerving impression that if you did, she would probably strip ya down in front of everyone, make ya stand on a box with your arms outstretched, place a black pointy cloth on your head and attach electrodes to your gels, just to teach you a lesson.

Upon arrival, the heat sears your pale Irish skin off and cauterises your lungs. After an hour on the tarmac you realise that your bags have gone on a holiday of their own. After a fifty mile journey inland to your 'beach side apartment' you realise that the travel agent has taken more liberties with his description than Brendan Courtney in a mickey factory.

In your matchboxed sized 'apartment' the mattress has more stains on it than Doctor Marie Cassidy's overalls, and you can't move without stepping on a cockroach or a used jonnie. The balcony 'with views' consists of a wonderful vista of giant cranes, diggers and builders' cracks.

The only relief from utter boredom and heat stroke is to dive into the tiny pool laced with the piss of a thousand over-excited children.

Only thirteen days to go!

BALLYDUNG BOYS GO WILD

The best holiday that Ballydungers ever had was with the Captain, who took the Cub Scouts to sunny Spain in the summer of 1937. They stayed in caves at night and during daylight hours went adventuring and shooting people in a lovely place called Guadalajara. It was great craic and a distraction from the mundane life they led back in Ballydung. It was a few months later that their parents realised that the Captain had taken them to fight as mercenaries in the Spanish Civil War.

A few years later when the Captain was fighting for the Germans, he invited us to go on a hiking holiday into Warsaw, but we had already booked into Mosney.

Another holiday we remember was back in 1972. We were quite the swingers back then and no woman was safe. With a prophylactic in one pocket and a packet of Silvermints in the other, the O'Leprosy brothers were heading to Salthill for a 'riding' holiday. We remember Mrs. O'Toole's B&B. She was a big beard of a woman who could make a sailor puke with her colourful language. The doors were locked at 9.30 sharp at night and her 'no women in the rooms' policy was enforced under threat of mickey mutilation. Naturally we saw all this

as a challenge and tried to sneak birds* back for a bit of jiggery pokery.

Every day of those two weeks was magical. It began with Mrs. O'Toole's fry–up which had claimed both her husbands and would put hairs on your chest, and indeed Mrs. O'Toole was living testament to this. Then we went sniffing down at the seafront for any swimsuit action. Occasionally ya might get lucky and you could crack one off whilst pretending to change under your towel. Then it was down to the amusements to loiter, and hopefully get a glimpse up a skirt from a vantage point under the waltzer. We sometimes paid the young fella working it, to speed it up a little faster if a bird in a mini-skirt got on. Tuppence would complete your afternoon with a go on the 'What the Butler Saw' machine.

In the evenings there might be a dance, or at the very least a ceili, and if there was anywhere you might get mickey action this was it. Over the two wonderful weeks we got our end away with birds of all shapes and sizes, and our mickeys were red raw from riding and from getting caught** riding by Mrs.O'Toole.

We often had a 99 ice cream for lunch, and after a hard night 'doing it' the flake wasn't the only thing stuck in the cone. It was a great Summer and we both came home to Ballydung, broke and infected, but with a head full of memories.

HALF BORED

You would imagine that holidaying in our own country would be a less risky option than traveling to a country you've never seen, never mind heard of. But you'd be wrong! Cockroaches and dysentry may well be a welcome respite after a holiday in Ireland, as there are many pitfalls to an Irish holiday.

The first is the weather. It's a meteorological fact (ask Martin King, he'll confirm this!) that the day you're travelling will be the hottest day of the year, and as soon as you open your car door at your destination, you will experience the wettest two weeks since records began!

The second misconception is that you actually save money by staying 'at home.' The local supermarket where you are forced to buy your provisions charges admission, and the prices are twinned with the gift shop in the Royal Hotel, Monte Carlo. 'Best before dates' have been replaced with more optimistic 'best before dates' and the fresh bread was indeed once fresh, long, long ago. The only filling station within a twenty mile radius is run by a man with six fingers on each hand and a son that barks. It has the highest petrol prices in the developed world. All the bars in the town, of which there are at least five, have separate prices for locals and tourists. And just when you think you can't be fleeced any further, you get the final bill from your holiday home agent

---

*   *Women were known as 'birds' all throughout the 1970's, courtesy of the popular 'Confessions' movies that came from across the pond.*
** *The punishment Mrs. O'Toole prefered was to use a cheese grater to your lad.*

with an unending list of extras that were added to your bill without your knowledge; towel rental, shower tax, soap duty and 'looking sideways at the locals' fines.

Another myth is that you are welcome in the town that you're staying in. You try your best to fit in, but don't try too hard, as the locals have a deep rooted hatred of all 'outsiders'. Behind the fake smiles and insincere platitudes lurks disdain and mistrust. Deep down you know you are about as welcome as a leper in a swimming pool. This coupled with the constant short changing, salmonella poisoning and the dirty protest-like toilets, are a big 'two fingers' to all visitors. They can't stop ya coming, but they'll sure as hell make ya feel bad for doing so. And if you dare complain about anything*, the entire village will hunt you and your family down, skin yis alive and stick your severed heads on the local Church steeple.

And finally, the biggest lie of all is that when the weather's good, Ireland's beaches are on a par with any beach anywhere in the world. Well, they are if ya don't mind a good dose of E. Coli from the overused eighteenth century drainage systems in every seaside town, or the odd surfers' sandwich**

It may indeed be occasionally sunny in this country, but it never lasts, as inevitably the North wind gets up ya worse than Elton John in a gym shower. And if you are brave or stupid enough to go for a swim, the water is so cold that your testicles retreat right up to your adam's apple and won't come down for three days until your body temperature returns to normal.

But by far the most embarrassing thing to happen when the sun shines in Ireland is that the entire Nation gets so excited by the big shiny ball in the sky, that in unison we all decide "Feck the sun screen, I'll make the most of it," which is the reason why after a 'decent' day everyone is walking around in agony looking like Simon Weston.

CONCLUSION

Now of course we live in Celtic Tiger Ireland, where holidaying all year 'round is the norm, even at weekends! In Éire we now have big five star hotels with golf courses and spa treatments.*** And if you want to travel abroad there are more destinations than you can shake a shitty stick at. And to top it all, the cost of flying is less than a sliced pan in a filling station.

As a Nation we are far more worldly wise than our ancestors, we have more money than ever in the economy, so there's absolutely no reason why we Irish shouldn't expect the best quality holidays available to anyone in the civilised world.

Bollix to that ya feckless rogues! You are dreaming if you think anything has changed!

The hotels might be bigger, but remember they are built in the same shitty towns, with the same begruding bastards that hide behind the same fake smiles they used on your parents and any chance they get, they'll fleece ya for every poxy Euro you've got!

As for travelling abroad! Bah! You still have to get the same poxy bus from Heuston station to the airport that has been running since the Seventies and stinks of Hen Party vom, or if you've got more money than sense you could park at the airport carpark a mere 17 miles away from the terminal, with parking fees costing more than most family cars or twice your actual holiday. The airport has never been busier or sweatier than it is now and more often that not you will suffer delays rivalling that of Brian Kennen's internment.

But there is at least one improvement over all the years of Irish holidaying; unlike in the Eighties when 72% of baggage went missing****, only 1% goes AWOL now. But make no mistake, fair traveller, as the law that Mike Murphy created, 'Murphy's Law' states; that one percent will undoubtedly be your poxy suitcase!

The safest thing to do is to stay in your home for two weeks. Stock the fridge up with snacks and booze, lock the front door and traipse around your house in your kaks pulling yerself off to repeats of 'No Frontiers.'

NOW THAT'S A HOLIDAY!

---

*   *In McClafferty's Bar, Scrote, three American tourists were scalped after*
      complaining that their ham and cheese toasties had blue mould on them.
**   *Ill-disposed jam rag..*
*** *Happy Endings are extra. But worth every dirty penny*
**** *69% of said missing luggage reappeared within five years washed up on*
      the Welsh shoreline

LUCY KENNEDY'S
TAN☀METER

From lightly sunkissed to melanoma – see how tanned you are compared to your favourite celebs!

Samantha Mumba
Mahogany

Anne Doyle
Nuclear Spill

Jordan
Jaffa

Lucy Kennedy
Sunset

Lorraine Keane
Light Rust

Glenda Gilson
Gamboge

Gerry Ryan
Gout

Pat Kenny
Natural
Woodstain

LUCY KENNEDY'S
TAN☼METER

Linda Martin
Dark Salmon

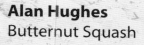

Mike Murphy
Marmalade

Alan Hughes
Butternut Squash

Twink
Tango

PODGE AND RODGE
IRISH CITIZENSHIP
IN A NUTSHELL

WHETHER YOU'RE MOVING TO IRELAND PERMANENTLY, OR JUST VISITING FOR A HOLIDAY, IT'S IMPORTANT TO FIT IN AS QUICKLY AS POSSIBLE TO AVOID BEING OSTRACISED, DELIBERATELY SHORT CHANGED IN SHOPS OR STABBED FOR BEING A 'JOHNNY FOREIGNER'. HERE ARE SOME ESSENTIAL AND VALUABLE TIPS FOR ALL OUR NEW FRIENDS FROM OVERSEAS:

CLOTHES:
How you dress depends on whereabouts in the country you live. There's no point trying to blend in dressed as a skanger if you're living in Tubbercurry. Similarly, if you find yourself working in Finglas, dressing like Jackie Healy Rae will do you no favours. Here's a general guide to dressing like a local:

- Dublin North: if you're unlucky enough to find yourself living on the capital's northside, trainers, tracksuits and gold jewellery are the order of the day. But make sure your trainers aren't too flash or you'll be mugged for them. Regarding skin colour, only one will do - mahogany woodstain. If you are not naturally dark skinned, apply as much fake tan as possible so you won't stand out.

- Dublin South: pastels will get you through most situations on the southside. Whether shopping for organic vegetables in the local Sunday farmers market (where you won't see a farmer) or on the golf course, a nice pale blue shirt teamed with cords and deck shoes will see you through. Just don't open your mouth until you master the ponciness or you'll give the game away!

- The West: only wear Aran jumpers if you are, or want to be taken for an American tourist. No one in Ireland - even in the west - wears Aran. Ever.
  If you are in Galway, a t-shirt with a witty slogan such as "Save Water - Drink Beer" or "Sex Instructor - First Lesson Free" will pass you off safely as a member of a stag party.

- Cork: one of the hardest places to fit in as an outsider. Like Dublin, they have skangers and ponces in equal measure, but are in a league of their own. Don a sweatshirt with "People's Republic of Cork" or "CCCP - Cork Capital of Culture Programme" or any other terribly clever pun on a fascist, communist or other oppressive regime and you'll fit right in with the infamous Cork arrogance!

- Midlands: if you're unlucky enough to find yourself in the midlands, your best bet is to head for the local main street clothes shop. Be careful to avoid any popular brands, and look out for shops named after people, such as "O'Byrnes", "Flynns" or "Kavanaghs", as they will usually offer a limited range of clothes from the 1970s. For optimum integration - ask to try on one of the jackets in the window which will be faded on one side.

DRINKING:
Irish and the drink - it's only a cliché because it's true! Sure, we're not all Guinness swilling bodhran players these days, but you still have to know how to drink like a Paddy if you want to fit in:

- Unless you live in Dublin, a man should never order a cocktail or spirit with a diet mixer. It sends out a very dangerous message.

- Despite the number of new fancy drinks and beers in the country, "a pint" still means a pint of Guinness. So if you are asked to get someone "a pint", do not say "of what?" or even worse, chance your arm by ordering a Carlsberg or popular new Asian beer.

- Designated drivers don't exist in regional towns. Most people drive home drunk or just sleep in the bar.

ACCEPTABLE DRINKS TO SERVE IN THE HOME BY TYPE:

- City ponce: Campari, wine, G&T.

- Farmer: pint of whiskey, poteen.

- Skanger: Dutch Gold, Bacardi Breezers.

- Culchie/ bogger: home brew, Tia Maria.

THE IRISH POST OFFICE AND HOW IT WORKS:

The Post Office has a special place in Irish people's hearts. We of course post our letters and parcels here, but also collect pensions, social welfare, pay our bills, make phone calls, get passport photos and business cards printed, and can even buy gift vouchers valid in several major shops. What a place you are thinking! But be warned, if you don't know how to use it correctly, it can become a bewildering experience.

- Not unlike The Queen's Guards in London, it is illegal for an employee of the Post Office to smile at any time. So do not be offended if when you smile and say 'good morning'`, they simply stare straight through you.

- As a new citizen or visitor to Ireland, you may have family or friends overseas to whom you may from time to time want to send a letter, card or gift. It is always advisable to bring an atlas with you to the Post Office, as their staff are renowned for their terrible geography, and it avoids embarrassment when they say "I don't have China listed as a country. Are you sure ya have the name right?"

- Never expect a traceable package to be traceable. It only leads to disappointment.

- On certain days of the week such as pension day, the Post Office will be very busy. However, it works this way - the length of the queue will be directly proportionate to the number of hatches closed. It is an old law still observed today. So if there are 20 people in the queue, there may be 4 out of 8 hatches open. If 5 more people join the queue, another hatch must close. Hopefully you can cut out and keep this useful guide, and the Post Office will soon become the bane of your life.

WHEN THINGS GO WRONG:

Ireland may seem like the Promised Land - we have two tramlines in our capital city, no rabies, and a job for everyone (if you don't mind handing out soap in the jacks), but sometimes things will go wrong. As a newcomer or visitor, it is important to know what to do in the event that something bad happens. If you are mugged, unfairly dismissed from your job or evicted from your house, snapped at by a surly bus driver, bitten by a cat, lose your car keys, get run over by a motorcycle courier or any other eventuality which leaves you feeling alone, unwell or in disbelief, there is one number you need to know. Not the Gardai, not your local parish priest or TD, not a friendly neighbour or the social services. The number is Joe Duffy's Liveline. Joe will be able to sort out even the most terrible of problems or injustices. Keep it on speed dial in your phone.

ST PATRICKS DAY GUIDE:

St Patrick's Day is an enormously significant day to Irish people living abroad. A day to celebrate their heritage, to meet with other Irish people away from 'home', tell stories of the heartland, and to rejoice in their great culture which has spread to the four corners of the earth. But here on Irish soil, the streets turn to rivers of vomit and rubbish and all we care about is making sure we still get a day off during the week if March 17th falls on a weekend. So a few pointers for all you newcomers:

- Don't bother with the parade, regardless of what town you are in. It's for children, tourists and pickpockets only. Real Irish people mark the day with a long lie in and making sure they get a seat in their favourite pub; so head in as soon as the doors open.

- When a tourist walks in to a pub, immediately break into song – remember, it's good for the economy. Recommended songs include "When Irish Eyes Are Smiling" and "The Fields of Athenry".

- It's a great day for entrepreneurs! You can sell anything on the streets of Ireland on Paddy's Day! From tricolour plaited wool to cardboard dancing leprechauns. Guinness with a bit of green food colour in it adds a euro to the price (but can kill if the wrong dye is used). Bunches of weeds from your granny's garden with a bit of tinfoil around them sell for a fiver a go as "shamrock". Give it a go - everyone can be Bill Cullen for the day!

Follow these valuable pointers and in no time, you'll fit right in as if you were a genuine leprechaun or member of Clannad.

Podge O'Leprosy
Ballydung Manor
Ballydung, Co Ring

September 8th 2007
The Banqueting Manager
An Fanni Mor Hotel
Church Street
Ballydung
Co Ring

To the manager,

I would like to make a booking for a party for October 2012. The reason I am contacting you so early is that it is me and the brother's joint 70th birthday and we wanted to be sure of getting a Saturday night. I'd say we would need a function room big enough to seat 300, plus room for a band and dancing. We would also like unisex toilets on the night.

Please let me know availability as soon as possible.

Yours etc
Podge

Podge O'Leprosy
Ballydung Manor
Ballydung
Co Ring
September

20th 2007
The Banqueting Manager
An Fanni Mor Hotel
Church Street
Ballydung
Co Ring

Dear Mr Ringer,

Thanks for your letter. The Maeve Binchy may be too large as we will now only need a room for 150 people max. I have my own thoughts on the menu so please advise if you can do the following:

Starter: Egg mayonnaise with Ritz Crackers

Main: Gammon steaks with pineapple rings and creamed potato

Dessert: We will bring our own Vienetta can you provide fan shaped wafers?

I understand you cannot provide unisex toilets so can we just stick a unisex sign over the ladies and gents?

Yours etc
Podge

AN FANNI MOR HOTEL
CHURCH STREET, BALLYDUNG, CO. RING

September 13th 2007

Dear Mr O'Leprosy,

Thank you for your letter inquiring about booking a room for your 70th birthday in 2012. You are quite right to book early as The Fanni Mor is a very popular hotel, and between weddings, jazz ballet recitals, leather goods sales and the annual fumigation, Saturday nights are booked up very far in advance. At the moment though, we can offer you any Saturday night in October 2012 in our largest function room – the Maeve Binchy Suite – which can comfortably take up to 350 people. There is a big dance floor and area for a band. Please let me know if you would like me to send on our menu options.

I'm afraid we cannot provide unisex toilets.

Regards,
Philip Ringer
Banqueting Manager
An Fanni Mor

Dear Bertie Ahern + 25

You are cordially invited to attend the 70th birthday celebrations
of Podge & Rodge O'Leprosy
on Saturday October 5th 2012 in the Fanni Mor Hotel, Ballydung.
Dinner and dancing and a whole lotta craic!
Tia Maria drinks reception at 7.30pm, dinner at 8.30pm.
Music by the Gee-Gees till late! In lieu of presents, please bring cash.
RSVP ASAP with a €5 non-refundable deposit.

Podge & Rodge O'Leprosy

AN FANNI MOR HOTEL
CHURCH STREET, BALLYDUNG, CO. RING

September 25th 2007

Dear Mr O'Leprosy,

We have several function rooms, and as your party has decreased in size, I would recommend the Adele King Room – it appears very small, but once you're in it, it's very spacious. The Adele King can comfortably accommodate 150 people.

With regard to your menu, we can certainly try to provide these food options for you, but I'm afraid we do not allow guests to bring their own dessert in. We have a wide range of desserts available.

Please advise as soon as possible if you would like to book this room as we will need to secure a deposit.

Once again, unisex toilets are not possible.

Regards,

Philip Ringer

Banqueti
An Fanni

Podge O'Lepros
Ballydung Mano
Ballydung, Co Rin

October 2nd 2007
The Banqueting Manager
An Fanni Mor Hotel
Church Street
Ballydung
Co Ring

Dear Mr Ringer,

After much consideration we have had to rethink our party could I book a table for three for the same date in your main dining room? It will just be myself, Podge and another ginger fella called Hector

Yours etc.

Podo

GUEST LIST + RSVP DETAILS
Celeb invitees
GRAINNE SEOIGE *said piss off*
SILE SEOIGE *said no thank you*
Additional Seoiges *didn't find any more*
SADAM HUSSEIN *apparently dead???*
TWINK (**do not sit her near Seoiges**) *said something very rude? Think it's a no?*
THE CORRS *said no as the invite didn't include Jim*
WEATHER BENNIES (**we need a few fellas, but not competition**) *said yes can we uninvite them?*
MIRIAM O CALLAGHAN (**allow 2 meals**) *said one of her kids ate the invite*
BERTIE AHERN + 25 *said government ministers cannot attend such functions*
~~RYAN TUBRIDY~~
CAROLINE MORAHAN **plus any amount of female friends** *no reply*
OSAMA BIN LADEN **invite returned to sender.** *No longer at address*
JOHNNY LOGAN (**to be sat away from stage area**) *can't fit into white suit long term dieting*
GLENDA GILSON (**NB do not sit near Katy**) *said sod off*
KATY FRENCH *said if it's not good enough for Glenda she's not going*
SINEAD O CONNOR *invite came back ripped up. Assume no?*
~~CAST OF FAIR CITY~~
GERRY RYAN *asked to see list of ladies attending first?*
10 **invites sent to PLAYBOY MANSION** *returned - insufficient postage on envelope*
~~MARK CAGNEY~~
ROSANNA DAVIDSON *Chris de Burgh replied upset he hadn't been invited? It's not worth asking him just to get her.*
NB: HECTOR O HOCH–HOCHAGH *RSVP'd with a yes but check who sent him an invite??*

BALLYDUNG GUESTS
FATHER FONDEL (**ask can he do non-religious Grace?**) *has a funeral that day*
GUSSIE BOLLOKIN (**will bring cheese and pineapple sticks**) *will be in hospital*
MARGO MINGE (**ask to make birthday cake**) *said she's not a fucking caterer?*
LOCAL COUNCILLORS – **allow 10 seats** *all said they didn't get our vote so won't come*

PODGE AND RODGE EXPOSED

failed exorcism and died in 1963. Once again the body disappeared from the grave. *NOTHING TO DO WITH US!* The Asylum officially closed its books on December 15th of the same year with the brothers O Leprosy now officially caretakers. Within a week they had changed the large wrought iron sign at the bottom of the lane from ~~Ballydung Asylum~~ to Ballydung *Bollox!* Manor.

Podge and Rodge were to remain in residence along with Granny, their cat Pox and the start of Rodge s primate collection. *R.I.P* *DIRTY FILTHY MONKEYS*

Pat the postman, now retired, remembers the change of address "Yer man Podge, that s the one with the straight hair isn t it? He thought he was Lord of the Manor. He expected me to ride my bike all the way up the lane to put letters through his front door, well, I tell ya, I left them at the gate like everyone else! And them parcels from Amsterdam and Copenhagen that the other fella ordered done my back in, jaysus, the things that have gone on in that place, only the Lord knows!" *Notorious SHITEHAWK*

Maintaining a building of such a size required money, so over the next few years Podge and Rodge set up a number of ~~illegal~~ *genius* businesses which they ran from home. ~~Illegal~~ bicycle repairs was Rodge s idea, but brought in little income and got him into hot water with Cycling Ireland, after an unprecedented number of injuries from bad spot welding and sloppy saddlery. Another ill fated venture was the Human Taxidermy service, which offered to preserve a loved one. However Podge is currently suing the Prague based Muerte Grande Humane company for stealing his idea. *FOREIGN PRICKS!!* *HOW FUCKING DARE YOU!*

It was by chance through their highly suspect

we both did her!

Ladies only B&B venture that they encountered Milandra Potter Pube, a television producer from Dublin who thought that Podge and Rodge would be good material for a project she was planning about bachelors living in the Midlands.

The documentary was never made but the idea of being on telly fascinated the brothers, especially Podge, whose ego and self importance was now at an all time high. He fancied himself as a modern day Seanachai and master storyteller. Mind you, he was always more Pat Ingoldsby than Pat McCabe.

True!

FUCK YOU AND THE GUY YOU RODE IN ON!!

RTE agreed to film the two boys in Ballydung Manor telling their tales (which Podge to this day insists are all factual!) and the Scare at Bedtime series was born in September 1997.
Many viewers tuned in to the late night slot and were amused to see these tall tales told with such vigour and salaciousness. The fact that they co habited a single bed only added to the charm. Incidentally the bed sharing, which so many find amusing, is not uncommon in rural Ireland, and it did nothing but enhance their appeal to a gay audience.

WHAT THE FUCK IS THIS!!?!?

Granny O Leprosy featured in the early seasons but was never seen on camera. She passed away violently in 1998, after her fourth, and this time, successful exorcism carried out by Fr Fondel who had just come back from the Missions.

Lovely man.

PODGE & RODGE'S
VERY CROSS WORDS

ACROSS

1. Just stocky IQ, for what you might have after a night on the beer (anag. 7,5)
5. Women are never one of these when you marry 'em, but soon become one. (6)
6. Could be benny Brian, could be our own lovely Lucy. (7)
7. A shite Coldplay song or the colour of unhealthy piss (6)
10. Podge and Rodges' surname (1'7)
12. "Show us your ___" a chat up line. (5)
16. ___ as two left feet. What people often say about Rodge. (3)
17. The ultimate rural guide to love as seen in this book (6,5)
21. Sounds more like a gay website, but was a band in the 90's (7)
24. Quote rat battles, for one of Podge & Rodge's favourite curses (anag. 14)
26. We used to love littering the country side with these, till they started costing 15c! (7,4)
27. Mad ginger travelling bastard with an unpronounceable surname (6)
28. A Scare at _____ (7)
29. Rodge's old monkey pal. (6)
31. Every woman wants to be woken up by one of these (4)
33. Tidy Remax for one of Podge's favourite hobbies (anag.9)
34. "Ask me_____". A popular Irish put down. (6)

DOWN

2. The last girl left standing at the dance (4)
3. Derek Mooney only likes blue ones, we like the flesh coloured kind (4)
4. One hipped fanny magnet. (3,5)
5. One word to describe Norton, Norris, Kennedy, and a host of weather bennies (3)
8. The surname of the finest sisters in Irish broadcasting (6)
9. Hide & Seek world champion (5,3,5)
13. Pop horny rag, for what we all like a bit of. (anag. 11)
15. Room, for a chap from Morocco. (anag 4)
19. We've brought shame on our country more times than any other by winning this contest! (10)
20. How did this corduroy-clad, jazz-loving, chatty buffoon make it into our crossword?? (4, 7)
22. Nothing compares to our favourite doe eyed, mad as a brush baldy singer. (6,1'6)
23. You can keep your King Burgers and McDonalds, this is the only place we'd eat a French Fry. (9)
25. Irish actor who appeared in one of our shows and nearly touched a mickey in a famous film. (7,3)
29. What we like to do in ladies changing rooms (3)
30. Podge's & Rodge's ill-fated feline friend. (3)
32. You can't knock a snack that's available in 2 or 4 fingers! Kit___ (3)

Ballydung Bugle F

WHAT'S ON?

SANTY'S COMING AND THAT MEANS PRESENTS! SANTY ARRIVES ON SATURDAY. SEE HIM ARRIVE ON THE BALLYDUNG SLEIGH.

To avoid a repeat of last year's tragedy, children please keep your pets well back from Santy's tractor and trailer!

Santy will be available for knee sitting and present giving in Freenum's pharmacy. 10 to 5pm.

Please note Santy must leave at 5pm sharp as he has to report to the Ballydung Garda station at 5.30 every evening.

THE PANDA ROAST: Traditional Panda roast on Saturday. Ping Ping will be available for petting in the cage under the tree up until Friday evening.

Music on the night supplied by the Athlone Gay Choir who will be traditionally run out of the town at ten to midnight.

Sticks available from Shiela's - €5 each

DJ Rick O'Shea from 2FM will be turning on the lights at midnight.

Please refrain from using the 'gay sticks' on Mr.O'Shea as we do not want a repeat of last year's beating of Jim Jim.

KNIT A FESTIVE JUMPER:
Ladies - here's a great pattern for your man this Christmas!

estival Supplement

CHRISTMAS SPECIALS:

Ho! Ho! Ho! Top up your 'Santan' and wow your relatives with a healthy Christmas glow! Three hour session for the price of one hour this week only! Call Brida at Orang-u-tan and make an appointment

GET YOUR TREE FOR FREE:

Buy a box of bananas and a box of satsumas and you can be in our draw and win a tree for free.* Only at Minge Fruit and Veg.
*Draw takes place December 27th.

GIVE A PERMANENT GIFT THIS CHRISTMAS – Come to 'Show us your Tats' – Special Christmas themed tattoos! Kids half price!
Appointment necessary!

BALLYDUNG MULTIPLEX CHRISTMAS SEASON:

Triple bills all this week
The Santa Clause
Elf
Halloween 3
Santa Claus the movie
Miracle on 42nd street
Universal Soldier
The Grinch
National Lampoon's Christmas Vacation
Last Tango in Paris
The Deerhunter
Spongebob's Christmas Adventure
Hard Boiled.

THE CHURCH
OF THE DUBIOUS MIRACLES
Mass Times:
Dec 24th Midnight Mass – 10 o'clock
Dec 25th - 9 o'clock,
10.30 with the Zimmer frame quartet
(please keep aisle clear for toilet emergencies and ambulance access.)

12.00 - The dousing of the witch.
Donations for the Old Folks lunch welcome until Dec 23rd. In date foods only please.

No dates or spicy foods please.

RANDY O'LEPROSY
(b.1972–) San Francisco

Randy 'The Meat' O'Leprosy, famous porn star (Men in Black Men, Bed Knobs and Meat sticks) turned gay activist. Ran unsuccessfully for Mayor in 2001. Lives with partner and famous 'penis caster' Frederico and their dog Travolta.

BULBOUS O'LEPROSY
(b.1905–d.1962) Hollywood

Disgraced silent movie star of the 1930's. Famous for his bulging eye antics alongside Harold Lloyd. Caught with a horse in a hotel room in the 1940's.

BONNY O'LEPROSY
(b.1530– 1572) Isle of Shoals, African coast

One of Ireland's famous female pirates, she captained the all girl boat the Lesbania, Her booty was legendary and men quaked and fell to their knees as the all nude pirate boat pulled alongside to steal their cargo. Legend has it she crushed 17 men's skulls between her thighs!

O'LEPROSY'S ARO

CHUCK LAPROSEY
(b.1919– 1964) New York

A soldier for the Giovanni crime family. Ran the 'Giovanni Tyre Company.' Was arrested in a 1932 on loan sharking and illegal bookmaking charges. Turned State evidence on Don 'Fritzy the Cat' Giovanni and went into witness protection until he was gunned down by 'Stammering Guiseppe Santorini' in a mall in Miami, Florida 1964.

CARLOS O'LEPROSY
(b.1955–) Columbia

Winner of 'drug baron of the Year' for three years running (2001-2003) Drugs used all over the world. Has own army and two hot tubs.

FR. LICTUS
(d.1969) Gambia

Originally Barney O'Leprosy. Second cousin to Podge and Rodge. Became a priest in 1953 and went to the missions in Gambia. Excommunicated in 1961. Became King of the GoOnMe Tribe. Has 15 wives and now worships the alligator.

MARY O'LEPROSY
(b.1800's) London

'Poxy Mary' was a prostitute in the East End of London in the 1800's. She spread the pox throughout the East End the Parliament and the royality. Remembered in the nursery rhyme Poxy Mary '"Poxy Mary had a scab and she gave it to the King, he had another scab and gave it to the Queen.'

CUTHBERT O'LEPROSY
(b.1795 - d.1830)
Pitcairn Island

Rumour has it that Cuthbert, not Fletcher Christian was behind the famous mutiny on the Bounty. Cuthbert settled on Pitcairn island, shagged the locals both male and female and died of jock rot in 1820.

HELMUT THOMAS VON LEPROSY
(b. 1874 - d.1941)
Wankendorf, Germany

Luftwaffe pilot and personal friend to the Kaiser. Crash landed in Ireland in 1915. Changed his name to O'Leprosy, killed a man and stole his farm whilst everyone was distracted by the ongoing war.

UND THE WORLD

LEONARDO O'LEPROSY
(b.1513 – 1544) Florence

Famous inventor and artist. He invented the 99, the toasted cheese sandwich maker and the suitcase. He was executed for heresy.

FUNNY BONES O'LEPROSY
(b.1874 -1915) Antarctic

Former school pal of Shackleton, self-proclaimed comedian was brought along to entertain the crew of the Endurance. Ending up being thrown overboard and is now more famous for his reputation as the most irritating man in the world.

LARRY O'LEPROSY
(b.1821 – 1860)
Van Diemens Land

Larry 'Three Legs' O'Leprosy was convicted of common theft in Galway in 1842 and was shipped off to Australia where he escaped and was a member of the notorius 'Bad Boys Inc' who sang by day and murdered by night. He was eventually gunned down at the famous 'Roo Bar massacre' in 1860.

The 'Talk' for Boys

By Father Fondel

MODULE 4:

KNOWING YOUR OPPOSITE NUMBER

GIRLS

Girls are different to boys, we all know that. They don't play sport and they're only interested in fashion and film stars. But they're also different in the way they are made. Not only on the outside but also on the inside.

All boys have 'manhoods'; you might call them 'willies' or 'mickeys'. Girls don't have these, instead they have an 'opening' — you may have heard talk of it in the schoolyard. It is sometimes referred to as a 'fanny' a 'vag' or a 'voovaa'. They also have breasts or 'boobs', which like cows are for milking and feeding babies. But woman also use their 'boobs' to attract their opposite numbers. I'm sure you may have noticed them, wobbling about under sweaters or peeking though blouses on cold days. Maybe you have noticed yourself staring at a pair of boobs for too long or pondering what a girl's legs are like above her knees and perhaps this has resulted in a hardening of your 'manhood'. But don't worry this is quite natural and if you concentrate on your prayers the hardness will go away.

Girls can be very distracting to a growing boy and that's why a solid interest in sport is of benefit, and a good biological knowledge of how a man and a woman work is important for the future. Because one day you will get married and will want to start a family and you'll need to know where things go.

KNOWING WHERE THINGS GO:

On your Honeymoon you may want to engage in intercourse, also known as 'riding' 'humping' ' doing it' or 'getting your end away' — this is where a husband and wife who want to make a baby, join together for a moment.

This is how it is done by happily married couples. The wife lies on her back with her legs open and invites her husband to insert his manhood into her opening. After a loving embrace, the man releases his seed into her flower, exits the room and allows the wife to sleep whilst the seed swims to fertilise her egg and creates a baby in some months time.

That's right, there is an egg or two hidden inside the woman, but these eggs need seeds to be planted in them. All boys have seeds waiting in their sacks, otherwise known as 'balls' or 'nads'. Only the strongest seeds will find the egg, so it is imperative to keep your seed stored away so it can grow strong and healthy. Wasting the seed is a mortal sin and is known as self-abuse. You might have heard of it referred to as 'wanking' 'tugging' or 'pulling off'.

The Devil will often tempt you by putting dirty pictures in your mind or seating you opposite a girl with overly large boobs. But you must be strong and resist the temptation to touch yourself.

A cold shower or a swift smack with the tip of a ruler on any trouser stirring will put an end to any impure thoughts that may be festering in your mind.

LEARN ABOUT WOMEN

Women are moody, that's a fact. Each month all women like to have some time to themselves and there's just no talking to them during this period. They might be short tempered and perhaps smell a little. But it's all natural and their mood always lightens after a few days.

HOW TO AVOID GETTING A GIRL INTO TROUBLE

1. Talking is ok, touching is not!
2. Never let a girl sit on your knee.
3. Never sit beside a girl in a dark place. For example, the cinema
4. Girls might wear make-up to entice you. Don't look them in the eyes.
5. Never sit in the backseat of a car with a girl unless your parents are present or the car is in motion.
6. Discotheques: the devil's playground and best to be avoided.
7. The drinking of alcohol whilst in the presence of girls is a double sin.
8. Avoid watching foreign films, television shows about African tribes or films by Roman Polanski.

...AND FINALLY

Despite the dangers, girls are human too and the day will come when you will fall in love with one and get married to have babies. So there's no harm in talking to your opposite number and seeing what their interests are. And if she likes the things that you like then maybe one day you'll be seeding her egg and be blessed with a baby.

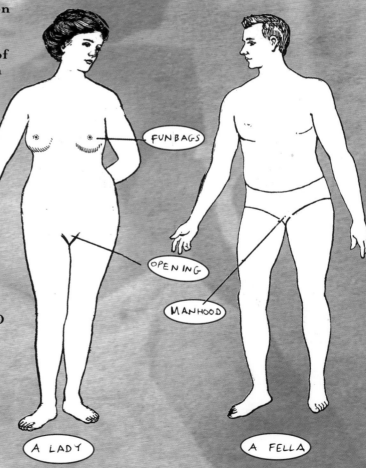

FUNBAGS

OPENING

MANHOOD

A LADY

A FELLA

Mayor Podge O'Leprosy
Ballydung Town Hall
Ballydung
Getting things done, for Ballydung
FANNYCAST
Call Rodge on 098 663 666
just sleeping
MAN TAXIDERMY SERVICE
oose your pose - eagle eyes - no smell
CALL PODGE 098 666 666
Dr. Rodge McGee
Mobile Gynaecologist
THE TAN MA
ALL OVER TAN APPLYING SE
WARM HANDS GUARANTE
INTIMATE AREA SPECIALIS
CALL: RODGE @BALLYDUNG
Couples catered for:
Your place or mine
CALL : SEXY 666
(Please supply your own Tant!)
Master Rodge
TANTRIC SEXPERT
Mr Podge
Professional Escort Service
You pay, I'll Play

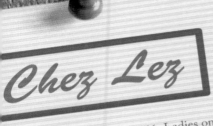

Chez Lez

t: Podge BALLYDUNG 666   Ladies only B&B
Ballydung Manor
s Only!)   Ballydung

Musty Memories
Dead Husband Clothing
Retrieval Specialists

Call:Ballydung 666 for a freequote

(Clothes removed from corpses if necessary)

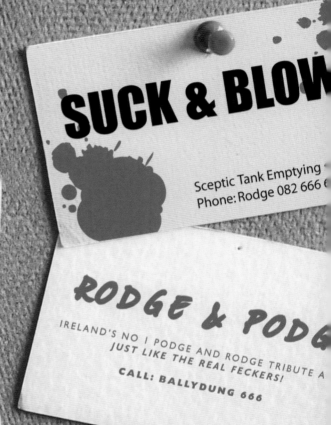

SUCK & BLOW

Sceptic Tank Emptying
Phone: Rodge 082 666 6

RODGE & PODG

IRELAND'S NO I PODGE AND RODGE TRIBUTE A
JUST LIKE THE REAL FECKERS!

CALL: BALLYDUNG 666

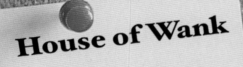

House of Wank

Employee of the Month
Master Bater

Need a hand call: Rodge

Sodom & Begorrah
All Irish Male Escor

Rodge Rua

SUCKY SUCKY
2000

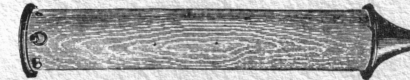

Place Mickey here

Arse baster

TITLE: A portable man relieving apparatus

INVENTOR: O'Leprosy, Rodge

PATENT GRANTED TO: Sucky 2000 Limited, an Irish Company, Ballydung, Co.Ring, Ireland

DESCRIPTION: This invention is a device to help satisfy every lonely fellas need wherever he gets the horn. It's fully portable and can perform a number of stimulations designed to get a fella off. However the 'Shanghai Duck Grope' will require three hands to operate. To be left up to the discretion of the owner of the device.

Rectal tickler

BALLYDUNG
BEAUTY SALON
Creators of the Pubic Hair Extensions

Ballydung's first and only beauty salon is celebrating its 10th anniversary. Yes folks – it's been 10 months since we got our licence back, so we're offering some mega deals!

New! Teeth Whitening!

There's no better way to get whiter teeth than our new caustic soda gum shield system. Get a dazzling smile in just 6 weeks with our unique patent pending "Caustic Smile" treatment*. **Available in Matt or Gloss.**

*Possible side effects include stomach ulcers, burns and loss of teeth.

Fat Friends

Are you flat chested? Do you have a best pal who has enough for two? Use your fat friend's excess flab to give yourself bigger breasts with our two for one offer! We suck the fat out of your chubby mate and pump it into into you! Everyone's a winner!

Bikini Waxing

Regular €20 - Brazilian €40
Hollywood €45 - Bundoran €55

Pubic hair extensions

Tired of the current trend for waxing? Try extensions instead!

The Elton John
(removable) €40

The Hector
(only available in ginger) €40

The Bono
(patchy effect) €45

The Richie Kavanagh
(specialised – ask for Rita) €5

Botox
The American Craze
Look like a Desperate Housewife on RTE

O'LEPROSY

PENUS MAXIMUM ERECTUS

Podge O Leprosy
Ballydung Exotic Meats Ltd
c/o Ballydung Manor
Ballydung
Co.Ring
12th March 1987

Dear Greenpeace,
I've seen ya on the news all the time, with your boats
racing around these whaling ships, and to be honest,
generally making a nuisance of yerselves. Have yis
nothing better to be doing?

You're always shouting "Don't be killing the whales", but
I don't understand the reasons behind your actions? Sure
they're only fish, albeit big fish. And we all like a
bit of fish, and if you're a Catholic sure ya have to
eat fish on Friday or you'll go to Hell. Would you like
me to go to Hell? Is that what you want me to do?

And another thing, what about Geldof and Spandau Ballet
singing their hearts out for the starving? Sure one of
them whales could feed Midge Ure and a couple of them
African villages for the rest of their lives! Plus
they'd have whale bone to put through their noses and
they could make a playground for the kids with a whale's
rib cage.

I just thought that you should know what the rest of
the world thinks, and that we don't all have nothing
better to be doing than sailing around the world, not
cutting our hair, hanging out of oilrigs and spraying
slogans on the sides of boats of fellas that are just
trying to make an honest living.

Yours

BALLYDUNG M

EVERY TOWN AROUND THE WORLD HAS ITS OWN STRANGE OCCURRENCES, HAUNTED HOUSES AND MISCHIEVOUS SPIRITS AND BALLYDUNG IS NO EXCEPTION! LET ME TAKE YOU ON A JOURNEY THROUGH BALLYDUNG'S MOST HAUNTED.

THE ONE LEGGED DOG OF SQUITTER'S BRIDGE

Back in the 1970's a farmer called McLusty had a terrible accident on Squitters bridge. A speeding driver in a black Volkswagen ran him off the road and fled the scene. McLusty lost his life that fateful night and his beloved sheepdog Hindu lost all but one leg in the accident. One evening in 1973 a black Volkswagen sped towards the bridge, the same one from years before. Out of nowhere, Hindu, despite only having one leg, launched himself through the windscreen of the car and it careered off the bridge. The next morning when the Gardai came across the car, they found only the driver, very dead, but it wasn't the crash that killed him, it was loss of blood as his legs had been eaten clean off. No one ever saw Hindu again, but if you're a VW driver, best stay clear of Squitters bridge!

THE BOG HOLE

Rumour has it that the bog hole on the Mullinasnot road has no bottom. In fact, drop anything into it, be it object or beast and you won't hear it land. They say that it goes all the way to Hell.

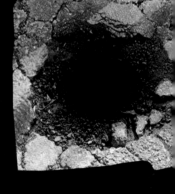

The story goes that Sean Og Hump and his brother Michael were in love with the same girl. Sean Og threw a note down the hole asking for help from the divil himself. And lo and be-hole-d didn't his brother drop dead that very minute. Sean Og went mad and threw himself down the hole.

THE KNOBBING SPOON

Once used in Ballydung hospital by nurses who needed to quell a man's fancy by rapping it hard on any urge he might be having. In 1895 the Matron lost her mind and went on a rampage slapping every man for miles around. That year there wasn't a single child born.

For safety 'The Knobbing Spoon' is now kept in a sealed glass box in the Ballydung Treasure room in the Town Hall.

OST HAUNTED

BY SHEILA OF SHEILA'S

To this day, every month of June a foul odour consumes the telephone box and it's said that if you pick up the handset at the exact time the lightning struck, you can hear the Stinky Man's screams.

OLD FLEM'S HOUSE

Flan Flemming was housebound with an awful condition. He had the most extreme case of the 'hack' ever seen by doctors. It resulted in him constantly having to spit as his nose and throat would fill to the brim with catarrh, and the only relief would be from spitting it up. His poor wife would fill buckets of the stuff, which she used to dispose of in the river. But there was a Leprechaun who lived in the river who was none too pleased. So he went to the house, knocked on the door and asked ould Flan if he could kindly stop disposing of his problem in the river. But Flan, whom at that stage was very cranky, spat in the Leprechaun's eye and slammed the door. Two days later the locals found Flan Flemming and his wife drowned in a house filled to the rafters with phlegm. And to this day, if you dare walk by the old house, you'll still see spit rolling down what's left of the windows.

THE PISSING GHOST

A tramp known as The Stinky Man would appear for the summer months every year in Ballydung and he'd make his home by the phone box at the top of the town. He was quite a menace, as he would use the one and only telephone box in the town as a toilet. One fateful night in 1967, there was a terrible lightening storm and as the stinky man was making a 'call' of nature in the telephone box, he was stuck by a bolt of lightning.

THE FELLA BEHIND YA

If you take a photograph in Ballydung Town square, at the left hand corner of the Jax, with the Town Hall steeple just over your head and as the clock strikes the sixth bell, a shadowy figure of a fella is said to appear right behind you. No one knows who it really is, but they say it's the image of the first ever Dunger.

BALLYDUNG SPORTING

This year, the year of our Lord two thousand and six, Ballydung celebrates a hundred years of sporting achievements. Ever since Donal McCracken came back a widower (but with a gold medal) from the 1906 wife throwing competition held in Glasgow, our little town has held its head high amongst Ireland's greatest sporting towns.

FRONT ROW (L TO R):
Mickey Rash,
Phil O'Hairy,
Bernard Box,
Dick Scratcher,
Lenny Pube, Tom Horn,
Fintan O'Mong

BACK ROW (L TO R):
Joe 'Phlegmer' O'Phlegm,
Peter Cyst, Larry Cyst,
Michael 'Mickey' Bulbous ,
Fisher Price,
Hoot O'Ganky,
Joxter McLaughlin,
Martin Roids,
Coach: Harry Barrie.

THE 1905 BALLYDUNG BASTARDS

The most feared hurling team in Ireland. Won the 1905 inter county championship. With the death of over seven players, it's a final that goes down in history as the bloodiest hurling match of all time.

Please note that nail studded hurleys were banned after this match.

CHAMPIONS

By Sean Scrollock

WOODY WOODIES (1880 – 1964)
GOLFING LEG-END

Before Tiger Woods there was Woody Woodies, who golfed not only for Ballydung, but for Ireland. After winning the Fred Daly trophy it looked like he was on the up and up. But after a tragic accident with a milking machine whilst visiting the Pubicon Creamery, his leg was literally sucked off and it looked as if that was the end for Woody. But he made a triumphant comeback a mere six months later with his false Hickory leg carved into a three wood.

In 1909, Woody took the Royal Portrush tournament by storm, beating off tough competition from Bertie Snowball and Tom Hood to take home the top prize of £11.

Woody's 'Wood' Leg has pride of place in The Jap Pub (formerly Keoghs)

MYLES STROKER (1916 - 1955) BOY RACER

It's every young fella's dream to drive fast cars, and every Ballydung boyo back in the 1930's wanted to be just like Ballydung's most famous boy racer Myles Stroker.

Everyone gathered around the wireless to hear the race of the century 'The Peking to Paris Rally 1937' to listen how our boy was doing along with his faithful sidekick and navigator Yung Hung Long. After forty-five days racing, across thirteen countries. Myles came in a respectable sixth place. He and Yung Hung Long came home to a hero's welcome and Ballydung was filled with ticker tape as he drove his famous Vauxhall 30 under a guard of honour of dung sticks.

Unfortunately he was run out of town with the same sticks when it was revealed that he and his navigator were 'involved'

MAY MCGUT (1963 -) BIG WOMAN

Despite the boycotts and scandal, the1980 Moscow Olympics were gold for Ballydung as our very own half woman, half mountain May McGut came home with half a dozen medals. Due to a growth defect, May had calves the size of a milk churn and biceps the width of telegraph poles. She broke five weight lifting records and was the first non-commie competitor to beat Korea and Russia in sixteen years.

Unfortunately her glory days were numbered as her medals were taken back after drug testing positive for androgenic steroids, testosterone, chorionic gonadatrophin, E102 and smack.

HUGH 'THE ROWER' SPITTLE (1959 -)

There was never a finer rower in Ireland than Hugh 'the rower' Spittle. Unfortunately his fear of water prevented him from ever rowing competitively but the people at the Guinness Book of World Records have him down as the fastest land rower. Clocking in at an impressive 7.2 knots during a field race in Northampton in 1973.

STUTTERING THOMAS NI GURK (1940 - 1966)

From the townsland of Flaming Hole came a true sporting hero. He managed to steal the title from Godfrey Littlestock – Knob as the British Isles 'Breath Holding' Champion in 1966. Despite a wicked stutter young Tom managed to hold out for a record five hours, two minutes and twenty one seconds.

Despite his last hour being discounted due to death, the post mortem revealed that he had indeed held his breath for a staggering four hours, two minutes and twenty one seconds, which beat his closest competitor by over half an hour.

His coffin was paraded triumphantly down Ballydung mainstreet. His headstone reads 'Thomas NiGurk – Breath Holding Champion. Died April 15th 1966, Still Holding!

Honourable mentions must also go out to Ballydung's very own up and coming jockey 'Lofty O'Hooligan'; our very own boxer Oxter McLaughlin, who's touring the world with 'The Rage in the Cage' fellas; hats off to the Pink Cocks, the gay badminton team featuring our very own Niles O' Length from Bumford and All Ireland dancing champion Nuala Goolick who is off touring the world with the All-Irish dance troupe 'Green Feet.'

And finally 'Up the Bastards!' for a win next year in the hurling!

BALLYDUNG

FOR A TOWN SO RAMPANT WITH NOTORIOUS BOLLIXES, SCANDALS OF THE LOWEST ORDER, MURDERS, SUICIDES, SEXUAL DEPRAVITY AND DEVIANT BEHAVIOUR, IT'S HARD FOR BALLYDUNG TO ESCAPE ITS BABYLON STATUS. IN FACT BALLYDUNG WOULD HAVE THE TITLE OF 'MOST SCANDALOUS TOWN IN IRELAND' IF IT WASN'T FOR MULLINGAR!

BUT INSTEAD OF KEEPING OUR CHEQUERED PAST BURIED, WE'VE DUG IT UP AS NOW WE CELEBRATE...BALLYDUNG BABYLON.

1963 – Farmer Solas 'Bulb' Crosby was literally ridden to death by his prize bull 'Arnie'.

1967 – Sean Manson of Manson Funeral Homes, Ballydung became Ireland's least successful serial killer after handing himself over to the police, claiming that he had killed over forty people. He had simply taken the names from his father's ledger and wanted some attention. The police decided to charge him with the imaginary murders as it had been a slow year for crime and he was ironically sent down for forty concurrent life sentences with hard labour, as it had been a slow year in the courts as well.

1977 – Road deaths trebled in Ballydung this year for what seemed like no apparent reason. It turns out that Mr Larry Mingus of Dump Crescent was convinced that the traffic lights at the far end of the town were more favourable than the ones he used every day, so he decided to swap the lights over. But in doing so put the lights out of sync and it resulted in an increase of 110% in road accidents in the area and thirteen deaths. Mr Mingus was eventually caught red handed as he attempted to reverse the one way street at the back of the church, in an effort to cut his journey to mass on Sundays.

G BABYLON

1979 – Local punk rock group 'Jizim' never had a number one hit, but became famous for performing both number ones and number twos on stage... in fact on the frayed cabling; resulting in the simultaneous electrocution of all the band members.

1988 - Etta and Ivor Coque were arrested by the Midlands Vice Squad in Irelands first ever bestiality sting. Under the code name; Operation Red Rover, the police were tipped off that some sordid activities were taking place in 'The Kennels' run by husband and wife team Etta and Ivor. The town was shook when they discovered that the couple who had been paid to look after their dogs were using the animals to satisfy Ivor's sexual gratification. One such act with Mrs Fitzgoolies' prize boxer was immortalised in the triple X film 'Screwby Doo'.

1990 – Japseye Hanley, from Two–Mile–Hole famously lost his mickey in an auto-erotic mishap involving a food mixer, a punnet of strawberries and two tins of golden syrup.

1997 – Scandal as Rodge O'Leprosy was arrested following an investigation into the sniffing of ladies' bicycle saddles. Due to the inclement weather at the time, he nearly got away with it, as ladies attributed their damp saddles to the rain, but when he was caught in the act by a local woman, the game was up.

2000 – Ballydung local Mickey Joe Girth died in the only recorded suicide by sandpaper. The only evidence found at the scene was a man-sized mound of human scrapings and a single sheet of eighty grade sandpaper.

A SCARE AT BEDTIME
THE GE

Turloch and Hannah Roids from Blackmanscock were heading off on their first holiday in years. Turloch had opened a new business, and for five years couldn't afford to take the time off. Meanwhile Hannah stayed at home to look after her invalid Mother who had had a stroke and couldn't get around by herself. She was a nice ould one and although Hannah never complained, she and her husband both needed a break. The fella in Sputum's Travel recommended Mexico; "There's sun, sand and Sangria," he said. "It's a great place to unwind." So they packed their bags. Hannah had made arrangements with Mrs. Splatter who lived at the end of the road to look after her mother while they were away.

On the morning of the trip they were all set to leave, but Mrs. Splatter was an hour late.

"Where is she? We'll miss our bloody plane!" Turloch was getting impatient, "Calm down, I just rang her, she lost track of time she said she'd be up in two minutes," Hannah reassured him. "Well let's go, she's got keys, she can let herself in!"

So they kissed Mother goodbye and left her watching the telly. As their car turned the corner out of their estate a boy racer came tearing round the bend and nearly ploughed into them.

"Well, that's a great start to our holiday," Turloch

TAWAY

A Tale of holiday woe by Podge and Rodge

houted, "The sooner we get on that plane the better." nfortunately the plane was delayed by ten hours. When ventually they arrived in Mexico they had a five-hour rip in the back of a truck to their hotel, which turned ut to be not much more than a corrugated shed. The ream holiday had gotten off to

bad start and it asn't going to get uch better. Their oom was small and indowless, the athwater was rown and they hared a bed with umerous nidentifiable nsects. The beach escribed in the rochure, as 'within alking distance is white silvery trand of heavenly

aradise', was in fact forty miles away and acted as a ewage dump for the town of Shitoga.

hen there was the cataclysmic bout of diarrhoea that annah suffered, and the four days in bed with a wollen lad that Turloch had thanks to a jellyfish

To make matters worse, after the first week their room was ransacked and all their stuff was nicked including their passports. It took them five days to get a temporary visa home from their so-called embassy.

When they eventually got off the plane in Ireland Turloch kissed the tarmac. "Thank God we're home," he said, "I'll never take another holiday as long as I live." They sped home dreaming of baths, decent food and getting back into the old routines. "I swear to ya Hannah, if one more thing had gone wrong I'd have lost me feckin' mind".

They turned the key in the front door looking forward to being greeted by Mother, whom they had both missed, but instead they were greeted by a swarm of bluebottles and the putrid stench of rotten flesh. There was Mother sat in front of a flickering telly, just as they had left her two weeks ago, rotting in her own juices, with stage six rigor mortis setting in.

Mrs. Splatter, the Mother-sitter had never turned up. She was mowed down and killed as she walked the short distance to the Roid's house by the same 'joyrider' Turloch and Hannah encountered the day they left. Mother lasted five days sitting in her chair unable to move. No one came to look after her, as no one knew she was there, besides her carer, who was lying on a cold marble slab in the morgue.

RUDUKO

RUDOKU IS EXTREMELY EASY: FILL ALL EMPTY SQUARES SO THAT EACH PICTURE APPEARS NO MORE THAN ONCE IN EACH ROW, COLUMN AND 3 X 3 BOX.

HERE ARE THE PICTURES. HAVE FUN!

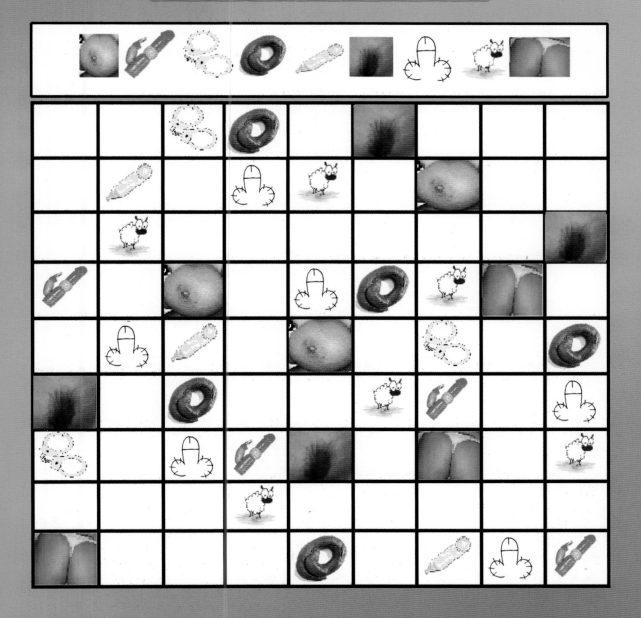

THE ULTIMATE
PODGE & RODGE QUIZ!

Q. What was the name of Podge & Rodge's pet cat?

Q. What did Ballydung Manor used to be?

Q. What are Podge & Rodge's full names?

Q. What crime was Rodge arrested for in 1997?

Q. Who was 'Granny'?

Q. Who is the boys' sidekick on The Podge & Rodge Show?

Q. You shouldn't dip your mickey into anything less than this!

Q. What was the name of the tribute band competition on The Podge & Rodge Show?

Q. What does Gussie Bollokin run in Ballydung?

Q. What was the name of Podge's greyhound?

Q. What programme ran on the other channel when A Scare at Bedtime was on?

Q. Who should you ring if you fancy slapping an arse and riding the ripples?

Q. How did Podge & Rodge's pet cat 'Pox' die?

Q. What is the name of Limerick CID's no. 1 detective?

Q. What school did Podge & Rodge attend?

Q. What was the name of Rodge's pet monkey?

Q. Who did Helmut O'Leprosy fight for in World War 1?

Q. What is the name of the travel agency in Ballydung?

Q. How many series of A Scare at Bedtime were there?

Q. But how many episodes have there been in total?

Q. What day is pensioners day at Labias Take-away?

Q. Who were the first two guests on The Podge & Rodge Show?

Q. Who won the Sham Rock competition in 2007 on the Podge & Rodge Show?

Q. Which Oscar nominated actor appeared in an episode of A Scare at Bedtime?

Q. What's the name of Ballydung's resident psychic and astrologer?

Q. How many days a week is Sheila's open?

Answers at the back of the book.

failed to be re elected.   *NO NEED TO MENTION THIS !*
The national broadcaster desperate to fill
a gap in the schedule, now that the
presenter had mysteriously disappeared and
denying any blackmail against them,
commissioned Podge and Rodge s talk show.

Podge at the time was quoted as saying,
"It s about time that Irish television had
some straight talking on it. Television is
at an all time low ever since they got rid
of Glenroe and Landmark. Sure, there s
nothing for anyone outside of Dublin 4 to
be watching and chat shows on at the
moment are all kiss arsed affairs!"

Rather than the bright lights of the
Dublin studios, RTE deemed it safer to
send a crew down and film the show in
Ballydung Manor itself. For the first time
the town of Ballydung benefited from   *# and what fucking*
something that the terrible twosome had *thanks did we*
created† Celebrities, audience members and *get?*
crew filled the town's B&B s, restaurant,
takeaways and bars. On February 6th 2006
a new era of talk show was born, with the
country's most unlikely hosts.

Despite complaints by bishops, politicians
and the elderly, The Podge and Rodge show
with the help of a young lass called Lucy *we both had*
Kennedy became RTE 2 television s most *her!*
watched show in recent years. *ever !*

The guests on the show included big names
like Shane McGowan, Brigitte Nielsen, *Tits!*
Stephen Rea, Sinead O Connor and The West *Mad*
Wing s Richard Schiff who all travelled to
the little Midlands town to be meted out a

Neil Jordans Bitch.

had her too!

uniquely Irish form of abuse from these two disturbed, yet frank, little men with a dark past.

But I do wonder would their popularity sustain if some of the more distasteful facts that I have unearthed were to become public? Podge is the biggest offender; for instance his barbaric treatment of his simpler sibling. From toe lopping (It is rumoured that Rodge may only have four toes left) to perhaps having a hand in Rodge's five fiancees mysterious disappearances. From illegal landfills and tax fraud to blackmailing guests to appear on the show (I have personally seen photographs of British comic Johnny Vegas in a compromising position; naked and smeared in dog food in a hotel bedroom with a red setter!)

Then there's Rodge and his pathologically deviant behaviour. Should a man with a criminal record be allowed on the national airwaves? From indecent exposure to suspected bestiality, from the restraining orders from nearly all female guests that have appeared on the show to five dogging convictions. This is a pervert of the highest order.

Yet, like their politicians, the Irish public tend to gift wrap their personalities and seem to dismiss their misdemeanours and applaud their achievements, even when the two are so gravely disproportionate.

So what does the future hold for the O Leprosy brothers now that

BLAH BLAH BLAH!!! (handwritten across text)

HOW DARE YOU! (handwritten)

WATCH YOUR BACK SONNY!! PRINT AND DIE!!! (handwritten)

Sputum's Travel

Arse Street, Ballydung, Co.Ring.
Telephone: 316 Fax: 317

"For fierce far-away holidays altogether!"

The New York Times

WRITER IN DEATH PLUNGE!

Police in New York are investigating the mysterious death of journalist and author Kurt Mingus, who was found dead outside his apartment building on 9th Avenue. His apparent suicide was unusual, as the 45 year old apparently leapt from a window, typewriter in hand with a rolled up manuscript shoved up his anus. A single page suicide note was found still attached to the typewriter. It simply read "I'm sorry for writing shite about people." The NYPD have not at this stage ruled out foul play and are following a definite line of enquiry.

Public Jax Scandal

OFFICIALS TO WIPE AWAY HISTORIC BALLYDUNG PUBLIC JAX!

Ballydung locals are kicking up a stink over County Ring's plans to bulldoze Ballydung's famous 'Jax' in a bid to rejuvenate the town square. "This is an abomination" said Sheila of Sheila's "Where are people going to shit now? This jax has been here since the town first came about, and generations, even Presidents have shat in our jax. We're proud of it and I think it's disgraceful what they're trying to do. They'll probably stick an apartment block up; sure isn't that what they're doing everywhere!"

DIRTY PROTEST

The Ballydung Bugle can report that a bunch of locals are so incensed by the possible loss of this historic bog, that they are planning a dirty protest. "I'll shit on their doorsteps, their cars and their heads if I have to" said one angry protestor.

"This could be the oldest jax in the world and they're planning to tear it down." Another disgruntled jax fan said. "If shite could talk, the stories it could tell. Do they even care that Raquel Welch once dropped a steamer in there? I'm sure they don't!" proclaimed another.

But not all the locals were upset by the news. For every pro-jaxer, there's an anti-bogger. "In the summer months the smell is unbearable" said one. "I saw George Michael hanging around there last summer and I won't be going there again!" another said.

BOG BE DAMNED

The steaming debate seems to be far from resolved, and a council spokesman said. "We've already passed a motion and the jax must go!" further adding " Sure there's no sink and god knows when the last time there was toilet paper in there. It's a health hazard."

But this shitstorm is far from over and the future of the Ballydung Jax is an issue that like a five pound steaming turd, simply won't flush away without a helping hand!

Sheila of Sheila's

Podge's Diary

I haven't had much time for me diary over the last while, as I've been too busy interviewing people in the Manor kitchen. Who'd have thought it? Me own series on RTE — well, along with Rodge, but he doesn't bring much to the table. I said last year that if Ryan Tubridy could get his own chat show, then telly must be at an all time low so there was no reason why we shouldn't sneak in under the radar. So here it is — our first series finished, and the craic we had! And it wasn't all shite D list Irish 'personalities', nope, we even got zeppelin-breasted Jodie Marsh and zeppelin-bellied Johnny Vegas on as guests. I reckon we'll be back next year so I've already sent in me demands — I want a personal masseuse, a driver, and some light relief after every show, so we'll see if the big-wigs up in RTE get back to me.

Rodge is like a dog with a sore mickey at the moment. Mainly because he actually has a canine related rash on his mickey, but also because our show was the closest he ever got to women off the telly without them taking out a restraining order — in fact the closest he ever got to any woman at all. So he's going to have to make do with peeping through hedges over the summer and dressing up as a changing room attendant in Shaws Almost Nationwide again.

The feckin' Eurovision is coming around again soon — just when I thought it couldn't get worse than last year's ginger nuts the McCauls, they went and stuck Brian Kennedy in, wailing in his benny tones about Every Song being a Cry for Love. Every song he sings is a cry for a punch in the face as far as I'm concerned. Lock me up till it's over!!

THE O'LEPROSY TWINS

JOHN & SÉAN O'LEPROSY

CONJOINED AT THE EAR

LABIA'S TAKEAWAY

Finger Licking Great!
BALLYDUNG MAIN STREET, BALLYDUNG

Come to Labia's and walk in the footsteps of hungry stars!

HISTORY OF LABIA'S!

Established in 1941 by the Italian husband and wife team of Giuseppe and Louisa Labia, this restaurant is a much cherished Ballydung institution. Now run by the third generation of Labia's, the food is still as good as when 'Mama used to make it!' Cabinet ministers, rock stars, business people and drunks alike can be found at the counter waiting for fish bought fresh that week, and a bag of their world famous 'Juicy Labia wedges' all cooked in 100% animal dripping.

So why not drop in to lip licking Labia's and sample our fishy and meaty delights!

LOOK WHAT FAMOUS PEOPLE HAVE EATEN OUT OF LABIA'S!

Jackie Chan, Linda Martin, Richard Nixon, Frank Kelly, Tom Selleck, Charles J Haughey, Eric Estrada (from Chips), Richie Kavanagh, The Saw Doctors, Navan Man, Ray D'Arcy, Jim Jim, Nicole Richie, David Norris, Bernard Dunne, Oliver Reed, Roy Walker, Peter Stingfellow, Marty Feldman, Ian Ogilvy, The Chemical Brothers, Terry Wogan, Brendan Grace, the Australian Doors, The Bloodhound Gang, Steve Guttenberg, Joe Elliott, Pol Pot, Limahl, Chubby Checker, Leslie Grantham, Shabba Ranks, Luka Bloom, Telly Savalas, Richard Kiel, Freddie Starr, Amanda Brunker, Electric Eddie, Joe Dolce, The Buggles, Ian Dempsey, Janet Jackson, Bros, Barry Lang, Chris Evans, Pat Rabbitte, Ben Dunne, Brush Sheils, Scott Gorham, B*witched, Dick Roche, The Sultans of Ping, The Thompson Twins, Maria Doyle Kennedy, Colleen Nolan, Gina, Dale Haze and the Champions, The Radiators from Space, Ronan Collins, Gary Busey, Ted Bundy, Derek Davis, Mr.Crow, Eddie Kidd, Mark Cagney, Hootie and the Blowfish, Mick Foster, three of the Four of Us, James Garner, the Australian Morrissey, James Belushi, Fran Cosgrave, The Proclaimers, Bez, Gary Barlow, Keith Duffy, The Australian Carter Twins, Duncan Stewart, Hazel O'Connor, Rodge.

Specials: Thursday
Pensioners Special!
Mushy Peas Juicy Labia Wedges (small portion) and Mystery Fish of the Day

€3.99

Special Kiddies Menu:
The Happy Box: Mineral/Nuggets Chips & Free Pencil and Rubber!

SHIT JOKES WE FOUND FUNNY IN THE '90s

ELTON JOHN IS WRITING A TRIBUTE FOR MOTHER TERESA.
HE'S CALLING IT SANDALS IN THE BIN.

WHAT IS THE BEST THING ABOUT GETTING A BLOW JOB
FROM A SPICE GIRL?
10 MINUTES OF SILENCE.

WHAT DOES MICHAEL JACKSON EAT AFTER HIS CHRISTMAS
DINNER?
AN UNDER EIGHT.

DAVID HASSELHOFF WALKS INTO A BAR AND SAYS TO
THE BARMAN I WANT YOU TO CALL ME DAVID HOFF.
THE BARMAN REPLIES SURE THING DAVE... NO HASSLE

WHAT'S WHITE AND WRIGGLES ON THE FLOOR?
COME DANCING

WHERE DID DIANA GO FOR HER HOLIDAYS?
ALL OVER PARIS.

WHAT SHOULD IRAQ GET FOR ITS AIR DEFENCE SYSTEM?
A REFUND.

WHAT DO YOU CALL A BLACK PILOT?
A PILOT YOU RACIST.

MICHELLE SMITH COMPLAINED TO HER
TEAM MATES THAT SHE WAS WORRIED THAT SHE WAS
STARTING TO GROW HAIR IN SCARY PLACES.
WHERE? THEY ASKED.
OH SHE REPLIED MOSTLY ON MY NUTS.

WHY DID BILL CLINTON STOP PLAYING HIS SAXOPHONE?
COS HE WAS TOO BUSY PLAYING HIS WHORE-MONICA.

MY COCK WAKES HER UP EVERY MORNING
By Fester 'n' Ailin

VERSE 1
The day I got married back in 73,
I took out me cock, sat it on my knee,
"What do you think of that me bride?"
She said "What a horrible thing, now leave it outside!"

VERSE 2
So my prize winning cock, she did snub,
I begged me bride "Just give it a rub."
But she hit it on the head with a frying pan.
And that's when all the trouble began…

CHORUS
My cock wakes her up every morning,
And it keeps her awake half the night.
I'd say leave it alone, it's a mind of its own
Now come dear, turn off the light.

VERSE 3
Now everyone in town knows my prize winning cock
For miles around they used to flock
To see him stand all erect and proud,
And he'd cluck all day and 'wow' the crowd.

CHORUS
But my cock wakes her up every morning,
And it keeps her awake half the night.
I'd say leave it alone, it's a mind of its own
Now come dear, turn off the light.

SPOKEN WORD BIT
Gentlemen be proud of your cocks, stand proud and
thrust them forward. There's no stopping natures
most magnificent creature
But a word of warning dirty cocks don't win prizes!
Now let me finish this tale of me, me wife and me
cock, there's a moral here for any cock wielding men.

VERSE 4
At what happened next you might be shocked,
For me wife one night took a knife to me cock,
Now my poor old cock, it is deceased.
But takes pride of place on our mantelpiece.

Ailin: Oh well that's the end of that.

Fester: Oh no, not quite

CHORUS
'Cause my cock still
wakes her up every
morning,
And it keeps her awake
half the night,
Now the other's been
stuffed, I've been
rebuffed
She says "Come here big
boy turn out the light"

Sputum's Essential Travel Phrases

Traveling can be a tricky and unpleasant business if you don't arm yourself with all the right information. Here at Sputum's Travel – the home of the discount honeymoon – we want you to be prepared for every eventuality when abroad. So we have compiled a list of essential travel phrases for the top destinations currently on offer at Sputum's, based on our previous happy customers' experiences. And remember, if you think there is a phrase we should include next time, e-mail Victor at sputumtravels@std.ie.

Iraq:
I would like to go straight back to the airport please.
Hal beemkanek mosa'adati tayarah min fadlak.

Amsterdam:
How much for both girls and the pony?
Hoeveel voor de twee meisjes en de poney?

France:
Your onion breath is making me sick.
Votre haleine d'oignon me fait malade.

Italy:
Guess what shape of pasta my penis most resembles?
Indovini che figura di pasta il mio pene assomiglia?

Spain:
Why are your women so hairy?
¿Por qué son sus mujeres tan peludas?

China:
I'm not eating that shite.
Zan jiao ping shite.

Sweden:
Your country is dull, but your ladies are better looking than ours.
Ditt land är tråkigt, men din damtoalett är bättre se än vår.

Germany
I'm not here to talk about the war, I'm here to taste some of your fine sausages!
Ich bin nicht hier, über den Krieg zu sprechen, ich bin hier, einige Ihrer feinen Würste zu schmecken!

Greece:
Stop it! I am not a woman!
Ztash! Nen eimai gunaika!

USA:
Does my bum look big in this?
Does my fanny look big in this?

Portugal:
Where can I buy a drink that isn't Port?
Onde posso comprar uma bebida que não é Porto?

Malaysia:
Could you train an orangutan to be a butler?
Bolehkah mengajar orangutan jadi pelayan lelaki?

Congo:
So you're saying you've never even tasted Um Bongo?
Alors, vous n'avez jamais goûté l'Um Bongo?

Sputum's Travel

Arse Street, Ballydung, Co.Ring.
Telephone: 316 Fax: 317

GARDA DICK ROSE SPEAKS OUT ABOUT THE ON GOING GRAFFITI PROBLEM IN THE TOWN.

The recent spate of graffiti is a grave cause for concern to Ballydung locals and law enforcement officers, in particular Garda Dick Rose who has had a personal graffiti campaign waged against him, with slogans around town such as 'Garda Rose is a mickey lover', 'Rose loves cock' and most recently on the back wall of The Lilliput Crèche; 'Rose = Homo'.

"Firstly, just because I'm not married does not mean I'm gay. The evenings that I've been spotted in the 'Iron Bar', I have been working undercover posing as an oily mechanic." said an upset Garda Dick, "I'm not proud of the things I've had to do to get a place in detective school, but I don't deserve this kind of abuse for doing me job." Garda Dick Rose went on to say that he and his housemate Garda Roger Browne have pledged to hunt down these vandals and give them a good seeing to, and punish them with the long arm of the law.

JIMMY D'ORGAN'S LEG IS MISSING!

Could all Gardai and locals keep an eye out for Jimmy's new wooden leg, which has gone missing…again!

KEEP AN EYE ON OLD PEOPLE THIS WINTER!

Ballydung residents are warned once again this year to keep an eye on old people this coming winter, as there has been a rise in incidents involving the elderly.

Close all windows and lock your doors, as wily old people will make their way into the warmth of your house and as we know once they're in and ensconced in front of your fire, they are extremely difficult to get rid of.

Never invite an old person you don't know into your home: There are a number of techniques that old people will employ to get into your home. Do not be persuaded by 'Would you be able to open this tin for me?', 'Can I use your phone to ring the doctor?' or 'Will you read the small print on me medicine bottle for me?'

GOOD LUCK SUPERINTENDENT BENT!

Everyone from the Ballydung barracks would like to congratulate Superintendent Bent on his retirement. During his forty years of service to the Ballydung community, Larry Bent still holds the record for most arrests in a single day and for his incredible ability to beat the shite of a suspect and not leave a mark on them! Good luck Larry! May the force always be with ya!

GARDA KARAOKE NIGHT

The annual Garda Karaoke competition was won for the third year in a row by Garda Dick Rose and Garda Roger Browne singing the duet 'Don't go breaking my heart'.

POINTS MEAN PRIZES!

Don't forget every penalty point endorsed over the coming months could mean a big prize! Let's try and hit the 1000 points quota before the end of the year and the Garda with the top score could win themselves a fantastic hamper.

TEENAGE CURFEW

A teenage curfew will be in effect for the Christmas holiday period. Hanging around, leaning on stuff, talking loudly, slouching and roaming around (i.e. In groups of more than two) and general messing will not be tolerated!

GARDA CHRISTMAS PARTY

For tickets for this year's party, contact Ban Garda Sheila Feelit. Price: €25 includes dinner, a go on the shooting range, dancing and a visit to Sergeant Santa himself.

GUNS FOR BALLYDUNG

Unfortunate news from Head Office as our application to arm all Ballydung Gardaí has been rejected once again. The measure that would have resulted in a lot less exertion from chasing after fellas and holding down drunks was vetoed once again.

GAME ON!

With five suspects currently in the cells, it's time once again for another Garda v. Suspects five-a-side football game. It will be held in the station carpark at 7pm Monday night.

CELEBRITY OR PSYCHO?

STABS in their EYES

FRED WEST OR MICKEY DOLENZ FROM THE MONKEES?

TED BUNDY OR JIMMY NESBITT?

HAROLD SHIPMAN OR HAROLD FROM NEIGHBOURS?

JOHN WAYNE GACY OR SIMON DELANEY

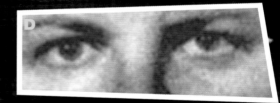

DAVID KORESH OR TOM CRUISE?

ANSWERS

A
FRED WEST

B
JIMMY NESBITT

C
HAROLD FROM NEIGHBOURS

D
JOHN WAYNE GACY

E
DAVID KORESH

BONDAGE/ S&M GEAR

Gents PVC posing pouch (one size fits all)

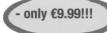

€6.99

Inflatable love aids (not to be used as life saving device)

from €11.99

Gimp ball (available in 2 sizes)

- only €9.99!!!

PVC Crotchless knickers (available s. m. l. xl)

€5.99

Stain remo spray

€2.99

AND IN OUR FOOD DEPARTMENT - LOCALLY CAUGHT FISH SPECIALS

Whelks

€1.99 a kilo

Schit mullet

€1.85 a piece

Brown trout

€2.99 a kilo

Dolphin steaks (Tuna friendly)

€5.99 for 2.

Smoked kippers

€4.99

OFFER FROM SUNDAY - CHILDRENS DIY EQUIPMENT!! GENUINE WORKING TOOLS IN KIDS SIZES.

Nail guns

€4.99

Circular saws

€9.99

Angle Grinder

€18.99

Paint stripper

€6.99 a tin

Chainsaw

€99.99

Extendable ladder (extends to 20 feet!)

€19.99

SPECIAL OFFER FROM THURSDAY ON ALL HOUSEPLANTS

Geranium

Hydrangea

Marijuana

Miniature Rose

all €7.99
including plastic pot!!

THE ULTIMATE PODGE & RODGE QUIZ!

ANSWERS

Q. What was the name of Podge & Rodge's pet cat?
A. Pox

Q. What did Ballydung Manor used to be?
A. An asylum

Q. What are Podge & Rodge's full names?
A. Podraig & Rodraig O'Leprosy

Q. What crime was Rodge arrested for in 1997?
A. Stealing ladies bicycle saddles.

Q. Who was 'Granny'?
A. The nurse who looked after Podge & Rodge in the asylum.

Q. Who is the boys' sidekick on The Podge & Rodge Show?
A. Lucy Kennedy

Q. You shouldn't dip your mickey into anything less than this!
A. Farmers Friend!

Q. What was the name of the tribute band competition on The Podge & Rodge Show?
A. Sham Rock

Q. What does Gussie Bollokins run in Ballydung?
A. A pub

Q. What was the name of Podge's greyhound?
A. Flasher

Q. What programme ran on the other channel when A Scare at Bedtime was on?
A. A Prayer at Bedtime.

Q. Who should you ring if you fancy slapping an arse and riding the ripples?
A. Roly Poly Rita.

Q. How did Podge & Rodge's pet cat 'Pox' die?
A. He was cryogenically frozen whilst still alive.

Q. What is the name of Limerick CID's no. 1 detective?
A. Detective Spunk Murphy

Q. What school did Podge & Rodge attend?
A. St Judas National School, Ballydung.

Q. What was the name of Rodge's pet monkey?
A. Spunky

Q. Who did Helmut O'Leprosy fight for in WW 1?
A. The Germans.

Q. What is the name of the travel agency in Ballydung?
A. Sputums Travel

Q. How many series of A Scare at Bedtime were there?
A. Nine

Q. But how many episodes have there been in total?
A. 150

Q. What day is pensioners day at Labias Take-away?
A. Thursday!

Q. Who were the first two guests on The Podge & Rodge Show?
A. David Norris and Diarmuid Gavin

Q. Who won the Sham Rock competition in 2007 on the Podge & Rodge Show?
A. AC-D-She

Q. Which Oscar nominated actor appeared in an episode of A Scare at Bedtime?
A. Stephen Rea

Q. What's the name of Ballydung's resident psychic and astrologer?
A. Larry Brown

Q. How many days a week is Sheila's open?
A. Every day! (Except Sundays)